Celebrating

REAL BEAUTIFUL
The Secret Energy of the Mind, Body, and Spirit

"A beautiful place to go and uplift your vibrations so you can create the changes required for magic and miracles to show up in life! Learning and applying the secrets exposed in this book will change your life in ways you never thought possible. Like a magic potion, all the ingredients needed to make healing, bliss, peace, success, abundance, and more appear in your life, are included. This book is a powerful gift."

—Tamara Gerlach,
Bestselling author of Cultivating Radiance,
Life coach and radio talk show host.

"What a tremendous and unexpected gift this is! Cindy has beautifully compiled a wonderful handbook for women of all ages and stages of life. She bridges the worlds of psychology, spirituality, energy healing, yoga, and health to create a very practical and powerful path to the realization of personal truth and balance in this busy, chaotic world."

—Jonathan Ellerby
Ph.D., CEO Tao Inspired Living,
and author of Return to the Sacred.

"Cindy Heath's book 'Real Beautiful: The Secret Energy of the Mind, Body, and Spirit' is a beautiful guiding light that helps you find and tap into your inner beauty and true greatness. Feel your energy rise, your positive vibrational field expand and your true life purpose unveil. Let Cindy guide and help you to honor yourself and your authentic journey—you deserve it!"

—G. Brian Benson,
Award-Winning self-help author/filmmaker
and inspiration advocate.

"Cindy is a tremendous spirit and enlightened teacher. Her passion for Kundalini Yoga and Energy Medicine is infectious and inspires others to live in their highest power. It has been a joy and honor to express her vision through the illustrations in the book!"

—Emily Brickel,
published illustrator
@ www.EmilyBrickel.com.

"Cindy shines as she lovingly presents the unlimited potential of spirit, magic, and miracles while living in tune with the energy and teachings in all that is REAL Beautiful!"

—Katrina Hill,
Energy Intuitive.

"The majestic power gained from loving oneself shines through on every page of this wise and compelling book! Cindy teaches us not only to create beauty and healing in our lives, but to embrace the power, magic, and miracles that can be found in our daily lives as well. This book is truly a masterful work steeped with honesty, inspiration, and most of all, the ways to self-love."

—Gina Pizans,
owner of Two Women and a Trunk
@ www.twowomenandatrunk.com.

REAL Beautiful

REAL Beautiful

The Secret Energy
of the Mind,
Body, and Spirit

*Uncovering the Sacred Science Behind Creating Your Own
Beauty, Power, Healing, Magic, and Miracles in Daily Life*

CINDY HEATH

Foreword by:
Kristine Carlson, Author of the New York Times
Bestseller "Don't Sweat the Small Stuff for Women"

BALBOA
PRESS
A DIVISION OF HAY HOUSE

Balboa Press books may be ordered through booksellers or by contacting:
Balboa Press
A Division of Hay House
1663 Liberty Drive
Bloomington, IN 47403
www.balboapress.com
1-(877) 407-4847

Book Cover Design: Amanda McKee
Gina Gallo Yoga for Beauty Tips Photographs: by Ron Handrahan
Author Bio Photograph: Blue Iris Photography

All Kundalini Yoga techniques and Yogi Bhajan quotations courtesy of The Teachings
of Yogi Bhajan. Reprinted with Permission. ALL RIGHTS RESERVED. To request
permission, please write to KRI at PO Box 1819, Santa Cruz, NM 87567.

DISCLAIMER: The information contained in this book has been written for the knowledge and use of
the purchaser and are approaches to health that should always be utilized in combination with the advice
of a family physician and in union with conventional medical approaches when and if required. The
information provided in this book is shared to provide further options to support and maintain higher
levels of health and well-being. Consult your physician before applying any of these strategies if you feel it
is necessary. Remember to trust your intuition to guide you to the most optimum health plan. Sat Nam.

Because of the dynamic nature of the Internet, any web addresses or links contained in
this book may have changed since publication and may no longer be valid. The views
expressed in this work are solely those of the author and do not necessarily reflect the views
of the publisher, and the publisher hereby disclaims any responsibility for them.

The author of this book does not dispense medical advice or prescribe the use of any technique as a form of
treatment for physical, emotional, or medical problems without the advice of a physician, either directly or
indirectly. The intent of the author is only to offer information of a general nature to help you in your quest
for emotional and spiritual well-being. In the event you use any of the information in this book for yourself,
which is your constitutional right, the author and the publisher assume no responsibility for your actions.

Certain stock imagery © Shutterstock.

Printed in the United States of America.

ISBN: 978-1-4525-7926-9 (sc)
ISBN: 978-1-4525-7927-6 (hc)
ISBN: 978-1-4525-7925-2 (e)

Library of Congress Control Number: 2013946714

Balboa Press rev. date: 11/26/2013

Contents

Dedication

To my REAL Beautiful daughters—Laura, Brittney, Caity, Amanda, Becca, and Tessa: your very existence reminds me that magic and miracles are possible in life. Your light and love have healed and inspired me throughout our lives together. Keep staying REAL Beautiful in this world!

To my husband Brad: Thank you for sharing this magical life with me and for the honor and reverence you have given to me as a woman, wife, and mother. I am grateful for the magic and miracles we have experienced together because we believe in them, and for the constant source of faith, hope, and inspiration you have been to me. Thank you for being a good father and role model for all of our daughters to witness and experience. You have been a shining example of the love, healing, and inspiration that are born when women are honored and revered in society. I love you beyond any words.

The most beautiful people we have known are those who have known defeat, known suffering, known struggle, known loss, and have found their way out of those depths. These persons have an appreciation, a sensitivity, and an understanding of life that fills them with compassion, gentleness, and a deep loving concern. Beautiful people do not just happen.

—Elisabeth Kübler-Ross

Foreword

by Kristine Carlson

As a REAL Beautiful visionary, Cindy Heath guides her readers to heal all aspects of their lives, but most importantly, she offers a template for living in love with life that is in tune with the precious miracle of life itself. She shows us by sharing her own journey of not feeling 'good enough' (feelings that have besieged most of us at one time or another) and how she has returned, through self-awareness, to her highest, REAL Beautiful self.

What I love about this book is its romantic heartfelt tone as Cindy summarizes a path to wellness in the most holistic sense – it's the kind of wisdom that comes through an oracle of the ages. The essence of beauty, which goes far beyond the physical, is powerfully exhibited in its rarest form in these pages. It is the kind of beauty that has been well earned through self-discipline, self-love, guidance from the divine, and grace. It is the kind of REAL beauty that radiates from being lit from within.

While poetically written, you will find this to be a guidebook packed full of insightful knowledge on how to achieve living and being REAL

Beautiful. Cindy shows us that there is no separateness in mind, body, and spirit, although people unknowingly live as disconnected parts of themselves daily. Harmony takes place when we embrace and accept our true self as it aligns with the miraculous design of the physical body. Only then, will our highest, most creative energy be expressed. When the mind is used to channel the spirit through the heart and the body, then life itself becomes one miracle after another. Cindy shows us how even the invisible breath we take for granted is the mystical life force that allows us to be here. Our breath is the portal into *the now*. If we can surrender to receive life's miracles beyond the hardships and sorrows and live presently, then magically we become an open vessel to all that is REAL Beautiful, and we experience REAL bliss.

Cindy puts into words what is true about physical health when she writes: *"I have uncovered a deeper understanding of the way our physical body works in concert with the mind and spirit. I have come to understand that we are energy beings that own a unique power to influence our own health, healing, and experiences in life when we learn the ways that keep our vibrational level of energy elevated."* Coming to know the energy principles shared in the pages that follow this quote will help you find your way to optimal well-being and harmony in life. The body is a divine instrument that requires our most devoted care and attention so it can perform its miracles. It is the sacred temple that houses your spirit.

While Cindy notes many spiritual thought leaders including Wayne Dyer, Donna Eden, Gregg Braden, and Yogi Bhajan in this inspiring book, she is in *mastery* herself in the REAL Beautiful being she clearly embodies with pure elegance, depth, and grace. I want to thank Cindy for inviting me into her REAL Beautiful journey. I know YOU (the reader) are going to love that you were invited along with me.

Treasure the Gifts of Life and Love,
Kristine Carlson (www.kristinecarlson.com)

Acknowledgments

There have been some beautiful angels who have been at my side every step of the way in this magical book-writing journey that I want to thank.

Mom, you have been my guiding light through the darkness, and I thank you for revealing yourself to me from the other side. Although I have lived much of my life without you here in this physical world, I have been blessed to have your guidance and connection from the world of spirit. Your knowledge and use of energy to reach me shine like sparkles lighting up the moments of every day. They are a part of the stream of magic and miracles I have been so blessed to tap into. I love you and thank you with all of my heart!

Tamara Gerlach, your kind and giving heart is your genius. I cannot thank you enough for your ongoing mentorship and friendship throughout the writing of this book. Your radiance shines everywhere.

Kristine Carlson, thank you for the courage, beauty, and grace you express in life. I am grateful that our lives became magically and mystically blended. You have inspired and healed me in more ways than you know.

Thank you to my daughter Amanda for sharing her brilliant and creative talents on the cover of the book, the healing mantra, and website design to help bring to life the message in this book. Continue to express your talent and light to the world!

To my daughter Becca, who loves the written word as fervently as I do, thank you for being there to listen, guide, and encourage me in so many moments as I wrote this book. Your support was priceless.

To my sister Colleen, the beautiful creator, writer, performer, and voice behind the REAL Beautiful theme song "I Am REAL Beautiful"—thank you for your never-ending belief in me, in my message, and in *energy*. We have shared so many beautiful moments because of these things.

To all of my sisters; Sharon, Patti, Susan, and Colleen, thank you for the gift of your 'sisterhood'. It has meant so much to me throughout my life.

To every one of my six daughters—Laura, Brittney, Caity, Amanda, Becca, and Tessa—and to my son-in-law, Cam, I thank you all for your LOVE and the encouragement you have all shared with me throughout life and while I wrote this book. Cam, you have saved me from being exhausted by computer/technical concerns because of your exceptional knowledge. Brittney, thank you for your smile, innovative style, expertise in social media, and the sage-like insight you have for many things. These things make you sparkle in day-to-day life. Laura, thank you for your unique ability to rise above life's greatest challenges, and thus, you have become a shining example to me and the world, that dreams come true when we stay focused and believe. Caity, thank you for every loving and inspiring word you are so easily able to communicate; you are so good at this. It is the greatest light within you. To my Amanda, thank you for your peaceful love and light that shines every day. To Becca, thank you for your big heart and the love it holds. And finally, to my littlest angel Tessa, thank you for loving me and the REAL Beautiful Movement from your heart. You spread the word about it naturally in your way of living and being that carries with it a sparkling light for your generation.

I want to thank the Kundalini Research Institute for the honor to share some of the teachings from Kundalini Yoga as taught by Yogi Bhajan®.

I want to thank Katrina Hill, Donna Eden's beautiful assistant, for sharing with me Donna's mission—to spread healing from one person to the next in whatever way possible through her teachings—and connecting with me on a magical frequency. Your faith in me and this book, and the magical stories we shared, became the light that guided me on. The potential to reach out and heal expands exponentially when beautiful hearts like Katrina's and masterful teachers like Donna are not afraid to let go of their gift and share it with others.

I want to thank Rob Handrahan for offering his talent as a photographer and Gina Gallo, for being the beautiful model in these photographs (Yoga for Beauty Tips). I am so grateful for both of you. Your contribution has been such a beautiful gift to me. Thank you from my heart.

Emily Brickel, thank you for capturing the essence of who I am in your beautiful illustrations in the book; they uplift the energy and message in it even higher!

Thank you to one of my greatest and wisest friends, Marty Henderson. You have been a constant source of inspiration because you believe in me. You deserve love, healing, and abundance overflowing because of your REAL Beautiful heart.

With infinite and heartfelt gratitude I thank my husband Brad for his love and support in all things. Our love has sparked the manifestation of many beautiful miracles.

I give gratitude and thanks to God, the highest power in the universe. It is this awe-inspiring essence that allows me the privilege to experience the magic and miracles that are available to any one of us when we understand ourselves as energy beings. Thank you, thank you, thank you… Amen.

For Every Woman on Earth

The sacred wisdom, technologies, and practices revealed in this book will ignite your light within to outwardly manifest the honor, reverence, beauty, power, health, healing, bliss, peace, success, abundance, prosperity, and ultimately, the magic and miracles that live inside you—mind, body, and spirit!

When you understand who and what you are, your radiance projects into the universal radiance and everything around you becomes creative and full of opportunity.

—Yogi Bhajan

Chapter 1

A REAL Beautiful Movement

Shine like the whole universe is yours.
—Rumi

The universe has your back, always.
—Danielle Laporte

REAL Beautiful Shines

*T*HERE IS A RAY OF light inside a heartbeat pulsing across the vast and infinite sky above you. Can you see and feel it? Its humble presence can be seen and felt inside the core of your being if you are willing to stop long enough and learn how to blend in with the movement of this mystical and energetic wave. Its expansive power, relentless in its giving, retreats with the sights and sounds of the day that hide it from you. But still, it secretly waits for you.

It is a challenge in our Western society to link into the sacred science that replenishes the strength of our whole being— mind, body, and spirit— so we can be carried across the challenging oceans we face as women in our effort to recover the value and honor we deserve in life. The narrow perspectives, misleading information, never-ending pressures, tiring competition, and chaotic pace block our view from a beautiful and sacred door that stores our secret powers behind it. Many of you have been living without your powers for a long time because you are immersed in a society that has misplaced the key that unlocks this proverbial door which houses these sparkling jewels. I know many of you have no idea such supportive resources exist. These magic powers can help you let go of the pain and suffering that results from anxiety, depression, addictions, disordered eating, weight problems (too much or too little), confusion, unworthiness, lack of success, prosperity, and confidence or whatever inhibits your path to become the magic and miracle maker you were born to be. These intriguing powers store the essence of our greatness inside the infinite combination of potions and elixirs they can create from our own intention and vibrational energy. When you learn to speak the language of the divine universe, your mind, body, and spirit will respond in ways you could never have imagined. This is the message that should go viral on YouTube.

The REAL Beautiful Movement is all about spreading these beautiful hidden secrets that light up the powerful gifts inside of you and me. Like a mystical fire they spark the flame in the hearts of women across the world. You will begin to understand the sacred science that lives inside your physical body and is written into your DNA that you yourself control. You will come to experience the energy raising technologies that reach inside your cells, change their vibration, and cause higher energy to rise up, spill over, and blend with the chemical frequencies of the universe outside of them. You will learn about the chemical potions that create beauty, power, magic, and miracles in daily life. This book is the beginning of a sacred revolution that opens the pretty little gift box you and I have been living in, and unties the ribbons that keep us from rising up and shining like the protective universe is ours, as Rumi and Danielle Laporte remind us in the quotes that open this chapter. When you can become one with this universal power, you will experience what I call *living and being REAL Beautiful*.

Let Yourself Shine

How does a woman become REAL Beautiful?

- When she understands the science behind her energy being and in the universe around her

- When she knows the powerful secrets hidden inside her physiology, and is able to create a magic elixir of her own with the energy of the divine universe. By knowing and doing this, she unfolds her REAL self and creates a beautiful life from the potent insights combined in the sacred science uncovered in the REAL Beautiful Movement

- When she follows the uniquely created REAL Beautiful ways of living and being developed and shared in this book and offered when she joins the REAL Beautiful Movement and receives: free gifts, secrets delivered to her inbox, higher vibrations from a healing mantra card, an opportunity to take part in REAL Beautiful Retreats, online healing events, and insights that keep her informed and connected to the sacred and scientific technologies that increase the vibrational energy in and around her physical body... and so much MORE

All of these things help to...

- calm her anxiety and stress
- release her addictions (patterns of behavior that do not serve her highest health and well-being)
- balance the flow of her energy, weight, hormones in the body, and heath overall
- heal her depression and create bliss
- attract success and prosperity
- manifest her real beauty at a cellular level from the inside out
- open the door to divine guidance that delivers inspiration, purpose, and all the magic and miracles of life

The extensive list of transformations above is possible when you make the choice to be REAL Beautiful and learn to ask for them by name. The specific things you ask for as you apply the insights, practices and technologies become your own magic words to your own magic wish. With intention and a couple other ingredients, you will learn to make your own wishes come true.

Chapter 2

Enlightened Master of Our Time: Dr. Wayne Dyer

Miracles happen. Be ready, be willing.
—Dr. Wayne Dyer

Real Magic

D R. WAYNE DYER HOLDS A doctorate in educational counseling and is well known across the world as the "father of motivation and inspiration." His brilliant insight through his teachings in over thirty books guides us to the ways of living and being that have the elements required to create real magic in our lives, if we dare to imagine it is possible. Dr. Dyer leads us to understand some sacred and ancient wisdom that exposes the truth behind who we really are: spiritual beings having a human experience. Listen to and practice his teaching and you will come to realize, as I did, that you are so much more powerful than you have been taught to believe.

Outdated and illusionary mainstream knowledge that is passed on through mass media and social learning teaches us to believe in states of fear, struggle, depression, anxiety, unworthiness, lack of self-love, diminished confidence and competence, and scarcity. We learn to have no expectations to ever succeed or have abundance of any kind in life. Where are we taught to believe that magic and miracles can happen? This information continues to hide from many in some secret and sacred texts, teachings, and masterful insights that have existed for years. For millions more of us, however, the veils of secrecy have been lifted and the beautiful and sacred knowledge is pouring forth. Those who don't believe it may mock and laugh at those who do; those who do believe know it is merely levels of conscious awareness that separate them and the miracles from each other.

I often said to my university students, "There are so many things you don't even know that you don't even know." Never think that you have uncovered all there is to know about who you and I are and the unseen possibilities that could exist. Be open to learning and believing that new and brighter things can take place beyond the hardships and sorrows of life. This willingness is required to unlock the door to creating miracles in everyday life.

It is my hope to bring forth truth, comfort, peace, and light to anyone who resides in the realms of being that are filled with darkness. I have been there. Listen to the wisdom in a quote from Dr. Wayne Dyer's teachings on creating miracles in life.

REAL Beautiful Gift #1
Insights from *Real Magic* by Dr. Wayne Dyer

"The way to understanding is through your willingness to reach your own highest state of awareness, using that awareness to get your life on purpose, and radiating that awareness to everyone in your life. It is primarily a mental trip so powerful that it can affect the material world with its miraculous magical powers. But you must be willing to go within and discover it for yourself. ... This invisible mental trip involves dispelling some powerful misperceptions and arriving at a new set of knowings."

Honoring Dr. Wayne Dyer

I find it fitting to honor Dr. Dyer as the first of the "masters of our time" I'll feature throughout this book. Words cannot really capture how grateful I am that the powers that be guided me to his work. His teaching became a lifeline that soothed me in the dark and pulled me toward the light of knowing the sweet comfort of magic and miracles in life. I have taken these insights and blended them with a powerful concoction of divinely downloaded and sacred insights that have been given to me to create the magic potions I share inside the pages of this book and in my REAL Beautiful Movement. I'm introducing the idea that magic exists in life early in my book for a few reasons: first, to begin the transformation required for you to be comfortable with the topic, as it underpins every chapter in this book; second, because exposing you to this idea begins the process of infusion of the belief into every cell in your body; and third, to foreshadow the magic and miracles that will come to you as you come to know the secret energy and sacred science inside your human design and in the universe that I uncover for you in this book.

Synchronicity and Miracles

It was synchronistic that Dr. Dyer's book *Real Magic: Creating Miracles in Everyday Life* fell from a community library bookshelf to my feet almost eighteen years ago. I was methodically and systematically pulling books out from the bookshelf that day just far enough to expose the covers and titles and long enough to evaluate the book's usefulness. If the book had no relevance, it was easily and quickly shifted back into its place on the shelf. This efficient process I developed helped me scan through multiple books at a fast pace. The flow of this process became interrupted by a significant *thud* as a hard-covered book fell off the shelf onto the ground before me. It was a mystical prodding and message for me to take note of the book, as if someone else placed it in my hands on purpose. It was difficult to explain at the time, but I knew without a doubt that this book had made a grand entrance into my life for a reason.

From all of my research, study, and understanding of the possibilities for magic to show up in life, I had plenty of examples of the miraculous things that could take place from moment to moment in daily life, as Dr. Dyer teaches. As the book fell from the shelf that day, I had already been practicing and applying some energy techniques taught to me by a counselor I was seeing to support me through the loss and changes that were happening in my life. She was untraditional in her approach as she guided me to play with the energy in and around me. She was the first teacher who brought awareness to me that I was made of energy and so was everything outside of me.

I was delighted at some of the exciting things that were happening as a result of the further insights I was gaining on my own and from Dr. Dyer's book *Real Magic: Creating Miracles in Everyday Life*. I found a hundred dollars one day, and then interestingly enough, again while writing this book. I was finding parking spots up front in crowded parking lots. I bought a house without a down payment. I was offered a position in research that supported my life better as I adjusted to being a single mother. Roses showed up at my doorstep after I said a magical prayer given to me by my mother just before her death. Money showed up in my mailbox unexpectedly. Initially when I opened Dr. Dyer's book, I recognized I had unknowingly read one of his earlier books, *Pulling Your Own Strings,* when I was thirteen years old. A warm chill spiraled inside my body in that moment because I knew I had been divinely guided to his teachings. This feeling inside of me marked the beginning of my conscious connection to spirit, an introduction to a lifelong guru, but it also guided me to continue to seek out the higher insights and knowledge of many more experts and masters across time. As I combined all of these higher ways of knowing with my own personal sacred insights and experiences over time, I began to magically and synergistically create the changes I wanted to see in my life!

The Power of Intention

After I read *The Power of Intention* by Dr. Dyer, another great literary work of his, I decided to apply his teaching from that book and from *Real Magic: Creating Miracles in Everyday Life*, along with some of my own secrets and I set an intention to meet him. And so I did. When I met Dr. Dyer in Toronto in 2001, I held my copy of his book *Your Sacred Self* in my hands. When it came time for me to meet him, he took both of my hands in his. I told him I was grateful for all of the wisdom his teachings had brought to my life. He took the book from my hands and placed his signature across the title on the inside pages of the book, and then he looked up at me and said, "You have a beautiful aura." From one energy lover to another, I was honored by his compliment! I was also further awakening to a brilliant power inside of me that was 'outside the box' of conventional thinking, yet had me intrigued to take note of the mystical information I seemed to naturally be in tune with around me even beyond this book. I began to sharpen my senses to the world of energy that spoke to me in a language I knew many people around me didn't understand.

REAL Beautiful Gifts

After the intense research and study I completed on the topic of magic, miracles, sacred practices, technologies, and insights for this book, I have no doubt—just like Dr. Dyer and millions of others— that magic and miracles do exist in life. I am honored to share with you ten of Dr. Dyer's insights from his book *Real Magic: Creating Miracles in Everyday Life* to guide you to come to understand better how to create miracles in everyday life. These insights will show up as "REAL Beautiful Gifts" (like the one shared above earlier in this chapter) sprinkled throughout the book to symbolically reflect how miracles can happen and guide you to them in your own life when you apply the knowledge in this book. Honor and revere these insights as you do the other powerful knowledge in this book, and I guarantee you will come to recognize the miracles that I more fully understand at the level of insight I have reached so far. When we are all ready, I trust that even more sacred secrets and insights will be revealed.

Chapter 3

The Real Me

*If you knew yourself for even one moment, if you could just glimpse
your most beautiful face, maybe you wouldn't slumber so deeply in that
house of clay. Why not move into your house of joy and shine into every
crevice! For you are 'the secret treasure-bearer' and always have been.*
Didn't you know?
—Rumi

A REAL Beautiful Truth

*T*HERE IS AN INFINITE MYSTERY inside us that, once realized, changes us forever. We begin to create and manifest our being and our world as if holding a magic wand with unlimited miracles waiting to be performed. We feel powerful and connected to the voice that calls us back to the truth. We become wiser, and mind, body, and spirit transform and heal. Beauty and knowing flow in and out of every cell inside us and intuitively blend with the energy that dances in the universe. We hear clearly the voice of our innate goddess, who lifts us up so we can see the honor, reverence, power, and uniqueness our gender holds—as it was always meant to be. And then we know we have experienced what I call living and being "REAL Beautiful."

> *The universe and the light of the stars come through me.*
> —*Rumi*

My Story

I believe my mother knew all along, even before I did, that I was a healer at heart. I am grateful for her insight and her gentle prodding that inspired me to become educated in nursing before her unfortunate death in 1989. I have lived half of my life now without my mother in the physical sense of the word—but as you will learn in this book, I have been guided by her spirit since her death.

Although my mother guided me to the nursing profession, it has been my passion for caring and the desire to heal that has kept me studying and practicing in this medical field. Along this journey, I have come to realize that we are all healers, but only to the extent that we are able to understand the power each human mind, body, and spirit owns as a result of its nature and design. This power extends beyond our ability to heal ourselves and others. The same power allows us to create self-love, beauty, bliss, peace, success, abundance, and even magic and miracles if we choose. When we master creating these things in our lives, we experience living and being REAL Beautiful in mind, body, and spirit.

You are powerful, providing you know how powerful you are!
—Unknown

The Woman I Am

My twenty-five years of experience in the health industry as a registered nurse includes a lengthy career in hospital departments dedicated to family medicine and palliative care. The past ten years of my healing career have been focused on promoting health outside the hospital doors as a nurse educator for university and college students, and more recently as a women's health educator through my own Successful Minds practice. For reasons I understand more today than I did in the past—and as a result of all my personal experiences, formal and informal education, and the unique circumstances of my life—I have been called to promote and enhance women's health.

As a woman myself, a wife, one of five sisters and five daughters, an aunt, a girlfriend, a mother of six beautiful daughters, and a spiritual mother to a million more, I have experienced womanhood on many levels. I have witnessed and personally lived in a culture that doesn't honor and revere women, and I have come to know and experience the pain and suffering connected to lower levels of health and life experiences because of it, on both a personal and professional level. My mind, body, and spirit have been wounded through multiple assaults that denied me the respect and honor I deserve, and I have recovered miraculously and beautifully from it all.

Higher Perspectives

In my time as a palliative care nurse, I was honored to be the caretaker at the doorway between this world and the one of spirit for those who passed on to the other side. This reality and a near-death experience of my own connect to my continuing search to understand our human and spiritual levels of "being" better. I will share more about my near-death experience and connection to the world of spirit a little further on in the book.

I have held the hand of a dying woman whose final words to me were, "I never felt good enough," and looked into the desperate eyes of a fourteen-year-old girl near death from starving herself, as she searched for an ability to trust me when I told her she wasn't fat and that her mind was playing tricks and distorting her own truth. I sat with my own mother before her death; like an innocent child, she worried that she was not doing a good enough job to survive her devastating journey through cancer. I have counseled and shared countless conversations with women who continue to reveal to me how they do not feel "good enough." I believe it is a sad state of affairs that the very individuals who miraculously create life have the true essence of life and living missing in their moments on earth.

The opportunity to heal, to be healthy holistically, and to create all the magical possibilities available is hidden in the fast-paced, greedy, and unconscious society we live in. For those willing to be conscious and step outside the box of conventional thinking, a whole new world of powerful information lays waiting to be exposed. These are just a couple of the reasons I am motivated to promote awareness of the power the mass media, social learning, and cultural ideals have on women's health and life experiences. The lack of knowledge can inhibit our ability to know ourselves better as energy beings, protect ourselves from harm, and elevate our ways of living and being to higher realms where REAL Beautiful gifts sit and wait to be opened, if only we know where to find them.

Like a wicked spell cast upon us, the ways of knowing and not knowing that inform and guide our day-to-day choices lead us away from the beautiful gifts we deserve to have in life. All this happens without our consent. We must be aware and willing to raise our consciousness to levels of knowing that can elevate us to ways of living and being that make these gifts available to us. We must learn that we are energy beings and that knowledge, words, ideas, people, places, emotions, feelings, beliefs, images, and all matter surrounding us inside and out contain vibrational levels of energy that are constantly interacting to manifest the elements and details of our lives. These interactions create a level of vibration that causes a magnetic attraction to all energies carrying the same energy or force. Like a recipe, if the right ingredients are included, we can create a new reality for ourselves and the world around us. I will provide the formulas and ingredients that have the power to expose the magical gifts, or what ancient civilizations call the *Siddhi*, to unfold and be part of your life. Knowing how to receive these gifts is essential. Not knowing is no longer an option.

Synchronicity

I know we have come together on the pages of this book because of a powerful universal source that connects us. It brings similar vibrations together, and they magically align because of magnetic forces inside and outside of us, whether we believe in them or not. It is plain and simple science. The real magic is in knowing this really happens and then being conscious of it when it does. I continue to be awed every day by the events, meetings, and circumstances that show up and are perfectly aligned with what is taking place for me in my life. They always mirror the vibration I am living at in any moment. I know the culmination of every thought, word, gesture, behavior, belief, emotion, and feeling I hold has created the events and circumstances of my life.

As we become aligned with this source and gain awareness of the truth about who we really are, we see clearly the magical power we own. From this point on, we see ourselves and the world around us differently, with our new eyes wide open. This shift opens our mind, and our consciousness increases. We receive the magical gifts of the universe with our magic wand in hand, and we never turn back. We know the secret to finding this power is our willingness to look beyond the obvious, stretch further, inquire more deeply, open our hearts, and sit quietly and wait for the unlimited possibilities and vast knowledge available to us. Certain knowing makes magic and miracles in life real; not knowing makes real illusions of the truth certain.

Some Things You Should Know

I have written this book for women because I have seen a lot of unnecessary suffering in some health conditions and ways of living and being—suffering I feel could be avoided with the regular application of the insights, technologies and practices I share in this book. My lifetime attempt, across multiple health fields, to understand our human and spiritual essence from a more holistic viewpoint has enlightened me. I have uncovered a deeper understanding of the way our physical body works in concert with the mind and spirit. I have come to understand that we are energy beings that own a unique power to influence our own health, healing, and experiences in life when we learn the ways that keep our vibrational level of energy elevated.

At this higher frequency, higher levels of health exist, as well as a connection to higher states of consciousness. This higher vibration can cause our moods to lift so we are not depressed, calm our nerves so we are not anxious, fill us with confidence so we feel empowered, teach us to love ourselves better so we can embrace our own beauty, and guide us to know the power we own to re-pattern our thoughts, beliefs, and ways of living and being so we can feel inspired, purposeful, and renewed. As you experience the shifts in your energy levels, the tingles up and down your spine, and the experience of the unseen and unbelievable that comes as a result of practicing the strategies and technologies I share with you, you will mystically become motivated to protect yourself from anything that tries to lower your vibration. We live in a world in which the mass media, social learning, cultural beliefs, people and many other factors can easily bleed out this magical vibrational power we own if we are not conscious enough. These things are so powerfully draining to our energy systems that it is like being placed under a wicked spell that renders us almost powerless in some moments.

Chapter 4

Wicked Spells

She wins who calls herself beautiful
and challenges the world to change to truly see her.
—Naomi Wolf

In the instant of our first breath, we are infused with the single greatest
force in the universe—the power to translate the possibilities of
our minds into the reality of our world. To fully awaken our power,
however, requires a subtle change in the way we think of ourselves in life,
a shift in belief.
—Gregg Braden

Waking Up to Our Lost Power

*J*T IS TRUE THAT INFORMATION is energy. Every word, image, sound, aroma, emotional impact, and tactile experience is information that all of our senses and our brain assimilate to try to bring understanding to the world around us so we can navigate from one moment to the next. Beyond this knowledge, all of these things carry an electrical charge that creates a vibration that mixes with the vibration of our own mind, body, and spirit to become one final vibration—a balance between all of the energies. The information we take into our brains drives the feeling, emotions, attitudes, beliefs, and behaviors we have, and ultimately the circumstances and elements of the world we create.

For example, let's say you have taken in information about violence because you have witnessed your dad physically hit your mom and you watch violence on television. Unless you consciously manage this information by having thoughts and ideas that say *violence is wrong* or *I don't believe in violence,* or *I won't act in violent ways,* you will automatically behave in violent ways. You need thoughts and ideas to override the observed learning that has taken place because of your life circumstances. This is why we see violence passed from one generation to the next. We see the cycle of violence end when an individual caught up in it rebuilds the beliefs, thoughts, ideas, and erroneous knowledge stored in his or her mind with newer information that builds neural pathways supporting nonviolence.

What Vibration Does the Information You Meet Up with Hold?

Since everything is energy—even the rocks and flowers in your garden, the trees in the forest and the ocean that surrounds the earth—so is information. Becoming more informed transfuses your mind, body, and spirit with good vibrations, the kind that lead us to greater health, happiness, and fulfillment in life, but only if the information we receive is high-quality. The information in certain types of mass media and socio-cultural learning has a low level of energy that has the power to cast spells on us on a cellular level as they build the neural pathways, patterns and rhythms inside us that take over our beliefs and how we think, feel, and behave. This information can even send out vibrational energy that harms our health and the chance we have to create a beautiful life filled with peace and all of the things we desire.

Because our mind is designed to automatically absorb information like a sponge, we have to be the master over our mind. We have to decide what information we allow in and out. Otherwise, we become spellbound by the false and illusionary information that surrounds us on a daily basis.

Sometimes what we have been taught, is not true.
—Colleen Sidun

Unlearn

You have to be willing to let go of and more or less unlearn some of the knowledge you have obtained while unconscious and replace it with information that you consciously decide you want to keep stored in your memory banks. With repetitive reminders to the brain over a period of time, you can rebuild neural pathways to support the new information. This becomes the automatic information that your mind searches for while interacting with the world. Like magic, we have the power to align ourselves with information that carries the higher vibrational charge required to bring good things to us in life.

Examples of Low and High-Energy Information

Simply, high-energy information heals and gives us the power to manifest the good things in life such as; more happiness, success, prosperity, magic, and miracles.

Low-Energy Information	High-Energy Information
Anger	Love
Lust	Kindness
Hate	Forgiveness
Stealing	Peace
Lying	Compassion
Violence	Truth
Jealousy	Sacred words that are saturated with higher vibrational energy
Bullying	
Music containing low-energy words or vibrational tones that make us feel edgy	Lyrics/music that contains high-energy words and vibrations created by the instruments
Aromas that make us feel sick or nauseated	
Ways of thinking or behaving that make us feel tense or sick inside	Ways of thinking and behaving that make us feel good inside.

Lower levels of informational energy make us feel depressed, anxious, craving, confused, and angry and connect us to life circumstances that match these feelings. Higher or good energy keeps us confident, inspired, on purpose, and connected to the stream of energy that makes these positive events and circumstances possible in life. Knowing the difference between high and low energy is critical if you want to own the ability to draw beauty and all good things to you in life!

Our Magic Wand

It is in our best interest to avoid informational energy that easily steals our power from us, since it will cast its spell and remove the magic wand from our hand. If our power is removed, we become weakened and unable to uplift ourselves or anyone else. Our higher visions of ourselves fade along with our self-love, and we are at risk of losing the honor and reverence we deserve and instead become de-valued, lacking self-love, anxious, depressed and so on. This lower energy literally steals our life away on multiple levels. If we choose to wake up and snap out of the spell, we have the opportunity to experience the magic, miracles, health, and life that exist if we are willing to do the things required to obtain them. Of course, this is not what we are taught for the most part by our parents, in school or through other ways of learning.

I've seen many women who are so entranced by the spell that they are frozen and unable to move. The truth is, many of them have been under the spell for way too long. I think you will agree with me that the time is *now* for this spell to be broken. You have been hypnotized and brainwashed by the powerful suggestions related in the knowledge that guides you on a daily basis to be perfect, flawless, thin, half-naked, and large-breasted to be considered worthy in this life. The mass media, one of the largest information systems that should help us to navigate safely through daily life, fails us. It is designed by conglomerates to keep us weak and disempowered under a spell that renders us blind and subservient from repetitive messages that advertisers are quite adept and skilled at creating to make us feel "not good enough" as we are.

The messages and images created for profit devalue us and rob us of our confidence as they prod us to be thinner, prettier, smarter, and less wrinkled, with flawless skin. We are urged to expose and objectify our bodies if we want to obtain any ounce of acceptance in our society. The messages not only poison our minds as women, but they poison the minds of all the men who are exposed to them as well. The messages teach men that women should be all of the things listed above to be acceptable. As these messages and images day in and day out draw us further and further into a deep trance, we become obedient and conform to the imposed ideals and unrealistic expectations. We pass on these expectations to our female children, for it is all we know.

Beauty Myths

In her book *The Beauty Myth,* Naomi Wolf writes that, through her research, nakedness is equivalent to having no power throughout history for women, slaves, and thieves. She also states that "To live in a culture in which women are routinely naked where men aren't is to learn inequality in little ways all day long."

We learn very quickly under this spell, as these messages insidiously begin to re-build the chemical structures in our brain and send out messages that continue to weaken us. We become brainwashed of our inadequacy. We end up bowing to unrealistic demands and spend every cent we earn and every sacred waking moment we have focused on trying to uphold these unrealistic ideals. In the end, the advertisers get what they want: a constant source of revenue, because we keep buying their products or services to feel better. Women who can't afford to keep up lay incapacitated in their homes or hospital beds because they cannot buy their way through the illusion. Either way, we never feel better. Our health becomes dismantled piece by piece.

We can barely function over time as we face progressively deeper levels of illness that seem to sneak up on us and attack us like a thief in the night ... and there we fall on our knees, alone, afraid, worthless, hopeless, powerless, and broken. We are unable to move, and we call out in the dark for help with our muted voices and deafened ears. We are unable to even hear the voices or take the hand of those who come to rescue us. Our minds are so tainted, like those in a cult, that it is difficult to convince us that we deserve to feel better. Our fear, unworthiness, and lack of self-confidence keep us from believing there is a way out of this misery. Venturing outside the status quo or box we've been held in is too threatening, so we retreat with exhaustion and confusion.

Lives Lost

Some women never escape this darkened place, and some lose their lives. How many more lights will burn out before things change? As I write today, I am still mourning the loss of a fallen sister, Whitney Houston. Her recording of the song titled "Greatest Love of All" was one of my favorites when it came out in 1985. I was twenty-one years old. All of the lyrics were meaningful, but it was the wisdom in one line that said it all to me: "Learning to love yourself, it is the greatest love of all." Unbeknownst to me at the time, these words would underpin a lifetime search to understand how I might know and love myself better, so I could help others do the same.

As an unconscious victim for many years, I shared some of the descriptive attributes listed above. It sounds easy to say that all we have to do is love ourselves and we will know the greatest love of all, yet there was nowhere to look to learn how to do that in a society that hasn't taught us or provided any clues or knowledge to study and apply. Until fairly recently, the ways to self-love have been elusive. I personally believe that self-love is a critical component to healing and health, and there is much research to prove this. At the same time, women have been taught by society they should love everyone *but* themselves or they will be considered selfish or "not good enough."

Whitney's song reflected a need in me to know how to love myself. It was a synchronistic messenger sent to guide me to the answers to some of the challenges lying ahead for me in life. For Whitney, the song becomes an ironic calling card now that we know of the tragic lack of self-love she felt in her life. Even though Whitney knew self-love was powerful, she was not able to consistently uphold the ways of living and being that could strengthen her self-love so she could feel good enough and rise above her tragic circumstances, like many others.

The spell lives on, even today. But there is hope. More awareness is happening across the globe, and in time, women will overcome the spell and the media will change because consciousness will change. Everyone will know that the information we are fed is not true, and injury to women of this nature will be nonexistent. No one will be buying or selling any products that play any part in the casting of spells on us. We will be smarter because we will be armed with knowledge and tools to undo the damage to mind, body, and spirit—and to prevent us from ever falling down again.

At Whitney Houston's funeral on February 18, 2012, Kevin Costner, her costar in the movie *The Bodyguard*, had these words to say:

> The Whitney that I knew, despite her worldwide success and fame, still wondered, "Am I good enough? Am I pretty enough? Will they like me?" It was the burden that made her great, and the part that caused her to stumble in the end. ... I think

Whitney will tell you, "Guard your bodies and guard the precious miracle of your own life." And then sing your hearts out knowing that there is an angel in heaven making God himself wonder how he made something so perfect. Escorted by an army of angels to your heavenly father, when you sing before him, don't you worry you'll be good enough.

RIP Whitney.

How many more lights will burn out before things change?

In mystical traditions, it is one's own readiness that makes experiences exoteric or esoteric. The secret isn't that you're not being told. The secret is that you're not able to hear.
—Ram Dass

Breaking the Spell

We have heard for years that we don't even use 10 percent of our brains, and some ancient and newer wisdom supports these statements. But whether you know it or not, you are an energy being interacting with multiple other forms of energy in and around you. This truth is explained in plain and simple science, yet many people are still afraid to embrace it—or maybe some are just not aware that it exists. I think many of us have experienced living unconsciously according to the knowledge and information that surrounds us and is most repetitively introduced into our minds on a daily basis by all manner of outside sources:

- television
- newspapers

- billboards

- advertisements

- romance novels

- social learning connected to the family unit in our culture

- the sports channel

- reality television

- the junk mail that comes to the door

- the limiting messages received from school systems that continue to label and then negate the emerging spirit and possibilities of our youth and more

We have also seen the dismantling of health through illnesses like eating disorders, depression, and anxiety. Many women suffer from lower levels of confidence as a result of the overt, illusionary messages in advertising and mass media contrived to make women feel "not good enough," weak, helpless, and sexually objectified so that products can be sold and profits made.

At the same time, we are being affected because our mind is like a computer and takes into our consciousness whatever we allow, and whatever we don't monitor or edit. We learn from and react to these messages without consent, because it is the natural design of our brain to take in what it is fed unless we are consciously monitoring the information and deciding what goes in and what stays out. This is powerful knowledge and should make you think twice about the things you choose to become a part of *you*—or, in other words, your energy being.

REAL Beautiful Gift #2
Insights from *Real Magic* by Dr. Wayne Dyer

"And then there are humans, who have the ultimate awareness of choice. We can choose to function at a lower level of awareness and simply exist, caring for our possessions, eating, drinking, sleeping and managing in the world as pawns of the elements, or we can soar to new and higher levels of awareness allowing ourselves to transcend our environment and literally create a world of our own—a world of real magic."

All informational knowledge carries with it a level of energy. *You* choose the vibration that acts upon your mind, body, and spirit.

The Flow of Informational Knowledge

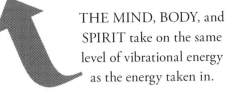

The ENERGY of the information we take on as truth infiltrates our cells and becomes a part of who we are, mind, body and spirit. It attaches to our beliefs, thoughts, feelings, emotions, and behavior—and connects us to similar energy outside of us THAT BECOMES THE ENERGY WE EXPERIENCE IN OUR LIVES.

INFORMATION from outside is taken inside our mind along with the ENERGY VIBRATION it owns.

CONSCIOUS OR UNCONSCIOUS REFLECTION takes place and we either learn without consent or with consent. Neural pathways begin to form.

THE MIND accepts the vibrational energy of the information consciously or unconsciously.

THE MIND, BODY, and SPIRIT take on the same level of vibrational energy as the energy taken in.

The Vibration Within Us

If you knew the powerful energy that information holds, you would monitor the information you allow to enter your mind and that of anyone you care about. As a parent, I have been diligent in trying to bring awareness of how our mind works, the negative health effects of some mass media, and the empowering news that we are in control of our own thoughts, emotions, feeling, actions, and so on. I have worked tirelessly to try to block the projected limitations passed on by mass media, culture, and educational systems so that my own children could be stronger, healthier, and able to activate their potential to achieve any dream they might have. It has not been easy, but the minute you take responsibility for the energy you choose to infiltrate your mind, body, and spirit; the manifestation of all of your desires awakens.

It took some work, and there were some things I had to unlearn myself before my children could, but I think the message has shone through. It's worth the effort to undo the damage and replenish your vibrational energy level so you can heal, experience your own beauty and power, and gain access to the magical secrets life has to offer you. It's not impossible to do. No matter how long it takes or where you are at, you can rebuild your energy being if you want to. I believe the greater the conscious effort, the greater number of secrets and power revealed.

Undoing the Damage

Self-talk describes the messages we relate to our brain through our own voice, whether out loud or silently. *Affirmations* are high energy words, thoughts, and ideas that are repeated by an individual that have the power to rewire our brains and imprint our cells with energy that strengthens us when they are repeated. I developed an educational video that reveals some simple and powerful strategies connected to our self-talk and affirmations that can undo the damage the messages of the media have inflicted. My goal was to support women's conscious path to higher health and wisdom in the mind, body, and spirit.

The self-talk and affirmations in the video will start the healing process as they build more supportive networks and channels in the brain while they raise levels of vibrational energy in your body. This knowledge brings media awareness, and if you practice the strategies I share in the video, they will also become your automatic ways of thinking instead. Check out the video on my website @ www. realbeautiful.ca. It's one of the many ways I will show you how to apply knowledge, technologies, and practices to support the raising of your own vibrational energy. This is just the beginning! Please view the video, and share it with every woman you know. Enjoy!

Chapter 5

Getting High

*You are a drug factory. The prescription that requires no drugs is
exercise, breath, and attention. Then all the required chemicals are
produced within your own body.*
—Yogi Bhajan

How Do You Get High?

*W*E LIVE IN A SOCIETY and a reality that is filled with challenges, sorrows, and pain—some of which cannot be completely avoided, but some of which can. Antidepressants are used by many in Canada and the United States, showing how hard it is for some people to keep their vibrational energy at a level that releases the proper balance of chemicals that normally exist inside the body. Yogi Bhajan informs us in his quote at the start of this chapter that we are like a pharmacy, and through certain practices we can activate and release chemicals to cure what ails us.

Many of us have been aware for a long time that exercising alone helps to release endorphins that lift our moods and make us feel calm. I will show you other powerful ways to feel good and go even deeper to share some well hidden secrets that I have uncovered that can make you feel high without the use of drugs. At the same time, if you want the high, you have to be willing to embrace the transformations required to get it. When you make some changes by applying the secrets and insights I share in this book, it will be easier, more comfortable, and a little more fun than you might think possible. Your consciousness will be elevated, your vibrational energy will shift, the need for willpower will be removed and you will be gently carried to the ways of living and being that cause a state of bliss to take over your life! All you have to do is be willing to try, and higher levels of vibrational energy will kick in and do the rest. Some secret, hidden, magical and invisible forces will come to support you as you transform. You will love it!

You have to be willing to embrace the things you need to change in your life—but you know this already. I have spent countless years trying to make the same changes as you. I am telling you, if you have been spinning your wheels—feeling stuck, hopeless, and lacking in willpower or whatever it takes to overcome the blocks that stop the flow of a good, healthy, and prosperous life—the strategies in this book will change all that for you. They will re-create you on an energetic and cellular level as they reprogram unwanted patterns, mind-sets, and ways of living and being so they can be released on a deeper level. The results feel like magic because there is something deep inside that takes over and inspires us to follow the directions our bodies give, and live in ways that uplift and empower, instead of breaking down.

Your beautiful issues in life will evaporate inside you, and you will fill up with wondrous possibilities. You will make your own drugs, medicines, potions, and elixirs, and design a REAL Beautiful life filled with all of the successes you care to map out. You will unhide the things that you cover up and release them from your energy being, knowing you can keep them gone as long as you raise your energy vibrations high. It's that simple. Let's address the hidden and buried pain and problems we have been afraid to look at, and infuse our bodies with higher levels of energy that will actually help us heal from the inside out and raise our vibration to levels that make us feel high on life instead of drugs.

In reality, the synthetic drugs people in our Western society use to feel better often end up making them feel worse. They clog up our cells and impede the flow of higher energy throughout the body. Just look at the commercials that try to convince us to add another antidepressant on top of the one that isn't working, to make it work better. Wow, it is difficult to know how we have been lulled into believing this. The joy of life, and the sanctuary you seek, can be found at higher vibrations. Once you learn how, you can raise the vibration in your physical body with your own physiology to experience these higher states of being. When you do this, bliss and the treasures that exist in other elevated realms of living will unfold before your eyes. You will learn how to find within yourself the things you want to show up for you in life.

Feeling High

I watched a video by Kris Carr, the *New York Times* best-selling author of *Crazy Sexy Diet*. She is a real rocking warrior for health and a master magic-potion maker. Kris faced the worst news possible in 2003 when she was told she had an incurable, inoperable liver cancer called epithelioid hemangioendothelioma. I see the acronym for this big long scary word as EAT. Interestingly enough, changing the foods she ate was one of the critical ways Kris halted and re-staged her cancer. She also added yoga, meditation, and visualization to her daily agenda to help empower her results. All of these activities can be used to saturate the mind, body, and spirit with high-energy vibrations. Kris shares high-energy nutrients with us on her website and in her newest book, *Crazy Sexy Kitchen*.

The high-energy formulas Kris applied to her life stopped her cancer in its tracks. We are blessed to benefit from the foods Kris guides us to and the ways of living and being she recommends to make health and healing happen. Beyond better health, her higher vibrational living has brought success, abundance, inspiration, purpose, and as I'm sure she would agree, magic and miracles. I love that Kris became the CEO of her own health and well-being. She makes me laugh when she becomes almost giddy about sharing a "green cocktail" smoothie recipe online at crazysexyjuice.com. She tells us how all the power-packed nutrition makes her feel high. If you want to read more about Kris Carr, please go to her website at crazysexylife.com.

I will not discuss nutrition as a way to raise your vibration in this book—that's a book in itself —in this book, you will learn to raise your vibrations by activating the secrets and magic inside your own intelligent physiology along with the mystical and beautiful streams of energy that surround you in any given moment. There are other ways to feed our mind, body, and spirit beyond food that are like potent magical elixirs that transform health and happiness in our lives like nothing else. It is up to you to decide which practices and insights from this book you will choose to create your formulas for getting high.

Staying High

Beyond the nutrients we take in through the food we eat, the thoughts, ideas, words, feelings, heartfelt emotions, beliefs, attitudes, and behaviors we own contribute to the chemical pharmacy we store inside of us. All of the energy that is contained within these things contributes to the sum total level of the energy you and I vibrate and radiate along with the universe. The vibration we make is a language that speaks to every living cell in our body and to the energy of the universe. What messages are you sending out? Everything that exists in your life in this moment is the feedback from the messages you have already written. Let's learn to speak the language of beauty, bliss, peace, healing, success, love, and any other desire you might have. It is time for you to know the truth that you are the creator of all of these things.

Staying high means we have to be willing to gain the knowledge that makes the things we desire happen. That means purging our lives of the sources of vibrations that drag us down to lower levels:

- mass media and advertisements that dishonor women
- television and magazines that feed our fears
- addictions that make us feel "not good enough"
- social learning, peer pressure

- some people and places

- parents, teachers, and social systems that are not aware of the insights I share in this book

- a variety of influences like wars, greed, stress, lack of higher consciousness, jealousy, resentment, fear, guilt, anxiety, competitive paradigms, loneliness, anger, isolation, depression, eating disorders, poor health, poverty, striving and so on...

I think you are beginning to understand the things that perpetuate lower levels of vibrational energy inside and outside of us. Feed your life the words, thoughts, ideas, feelings, emotions, images, and energy technologies that cause happy chemicals to light up and dance inside of you! Commit to doing what it takes to get high and then let the elevated levels of vibrational energy that result do the rest for you. You will begin to believe in your own power and a new and wonderful world!

REAL Beautiful Gift #3
Insights from *Real Magic* by Dr. Wayne Dyer

"Your emotions are physical manifestations of your thoughts. The joy you experience is located in your physical body, and the chemicals that are present when you experience elation can be identified and quantified. The same is true of fear, stress, anger, rage, jealousy, depression, phobic reactions and the like. These are all chemical changes that are taking place within you. You manufacture those chemicals in your own quantum pharmacy that begins with your mind. That mind is capable of literally manufacturing from scratch thousands of 'drugs' that show up in your body. Need an antidepressant or a tranquilizer? You need not necessarily go to the drugstore. Your mind can create exactly what your body needs."

Chapter 6

Our Energy Being and Energy Secrets

Everything is energy and that's all there is to it. Match the frequency of the reality you want and you cannot help but get that reality.
—*Albert Einstein*

Knowing Yourself as an Energy Being

$\mathcal{A}$s MUCH AS THIS MIGHT seem a foreign topic to some of you, the truth is, every single cell in your body is made up of energy that interacts with every other cell's energy in a magnificent and complicated dance, allowing us to exist from moment to moment. Rarely do we sit and wonder how we manage all of the interactions that allow us to eat, breathe, think, sleep, walk, run, and so on, from the inside. We only ever see the outside of who we are, unless we dare to search deeper. As with an iceberg, the tip reveals only a small percentage of the whole picture of what we are.

In my extensive search to better understand health, optimal living, and human existence, I have uncovered some sacred and beautiful truths about our human potential that not everybody is aware of. Once I experienced the balancing, magnetic, and healing power these practices had, and as I grew further to accept myself as an energy being, I was astounded at the results and compelled to share this information with you. I have made a connection to the mystical source of energy within my own body that becomes one with the matter, energy, and stuff the universe is made of (known to physicists and metaphysicists). I have felt the connection and oneness others have claimed to experience and a flood of inner guidance and knowing has filled every space of my being. It is difficult to describe until it happens to you, but be assured, you will know when it does.

The only way to make this happen is to begin seeing yourself as an energy being. Study the insights I reveal in this book, move forward with trust, and there will be no doubt you will link into this secret power as I have. You will be in tune with the frequency where everything on the list I shared in chapter 4 and all things REAL Beautiful, reside. The mystical and invisible forces inside and around you will be your guide to the ways of living and being that uncover even more secrets. This power is just one of the beautiful jewels that will light up and shine inside you as your vibrational energy adjusts and dials into these magical waves of energy inside you and the essence of the universe. The desire and clear understanding of how to achieve the wishes on your own list will be revealed.

My lifetime search to understand the human design and condition led me to assess and evaluate people and circumstance that take place in life on some deeper levels. In my years of palliative-care nursing, caring for those who were terminally ill, I have witnessed both finite and infinite aspects of human life as I watched over many in their dying moments on earth. These experiences, the years of research and study I have been dedicated to, the death of my own mother when I was twenty-five, my recent near-death experience, and the higher insights that have been infused into my being, have led me to understand life and death in some clearer and more comforting ways.

I have come to know the other side merely as a higher vibrational space you and I can join. This vibration is so high that our physical bodies cannot survive its full capacity, but we can experience smaller doses of the supreme beauty, power, healing and gifts the energy of heaven contains in the paradises we can each create with fragments of its sacred energy. The warm chills that pass through our bodies when these heavenly realms are touched identify our contact with them, those on the *other side*, and an opening in the mere thin veil that separate us from them. Although we may never experience the full expression of heaven and all of its glory until we enter it (the fullness of this realm) after our physical death, we can learn to speak the beautiful language that exists between these worlds, renew our ideas of death, and inspire a belief in eternal life. I am not the "Long Island Medium," but I have had some ongoing relationships with those who have passed on, as you will read in chapter 11. Until then, let's continue to explore your own energy and the energy of the world around you.

I will guide you in this book to see the importance of looking to the experts and enlightened masters so that you can step outside the status quo and the borders of conventional wisdom in the mass media and some social learning into higher knowing that uncovers the secret treasures that lay and wait for you.

Secrets Exposed...
Ancient Wisdom and Modern-Day Science

Ancient elite societies tried to hide the energy secrets I am sharing with you. Some present-day scientists are trying to expose them to us now, but not many are listening. It is time to listen closely. Never has there been a better time for this sacred knowledge to be revealed than now, when women's health is rapidly declining because of the misguided illusions related in the mass media and social learning. So powerful is this knowledge that it means the difference between life and death, health and illness, light and dark, peace and chaos, self-love and self-hatred, forgiveness and resentment, inspiration and depression, success and failure, poverty and abundance. All the secrets and gifts shown to me, one by one, over a lifetime of research and practice, are gathered together in this one sacred place to help clear the path to your higher vibrational self and your highest power more quickly. Please pass on these precious gems to every woman you know and love. Teach them to your daughters, sisters, nieces, grandmothers, and best friends. As I alluded to earlier, these are gifts so powerful you will understand the meaning of the word *siddhi* ("magical gift"), as the ancient elite did, and you will wave your magic wand and start living and being the REAL Beautiful goddess you were born to be.

What's Ahead?

I have had some profound experiences as a result of understanding myself as an energy being. Within these experiences, I have uncovered some beautiful and sacred ways for women to rise out of the pretty pink boxes they hide inside and open themselves up to the beauty and miracles their lives were meant to contain. Once again, I urge you to see the importance of looking to the experts and masters that surround us in life, one of which is *you,* so we can keep creating the life we dream about in the precious moments available in every day.

I have learned all of what I share from these insightful texts and masters and the higher insights that are given out like gifts for this effort. I see the gifts as messages telling me I am heading in the right direction in my search for understanding. We will learn soon that spiritual masters have told us that our seeking should be rewarded with new understanding of the mysteries of life. To find these hidden gems and jewels, it makes sense that you will have to seek outside of the knowledge you already know— mass media, elementary and higher educational systems, social learning, and so on. You have already applied this knowledge to make the life you presently live in. If your life doesn't include high levels of bliss, peace, inspiration, abundance, success and the magic you wish for, then the knowledge you build your life upon is not working. The knowledge that works is hidden in higher vibrational energy, secret scrolls, sacred texts and higher levels of consciousness that have all been carefully and insightfully recorded across the ages.

Gleaning from the Experts

One of the reasons I choose to apply the knowledge of experts in their fields of study to my life is because I know that the countless hours they have already spent discovering and knowing something— as a result of a passion and purpose that drives their desire to do so—reveal a far richer and truer understanding than any one of us could manage on our own, unless we studied to the same extent. It is up to every individual to decide which experts are the ones that are worthy of time or effort. You have to trust your own inner voice to guide you to the information that reveals the truth to you. No one else can do this for you. I ask that you open your mind to understanding yourself as an energy being, as it has been known even in ancient civilizations way before you and I ever existed. My own experience in knowing myself as an energy being has allowed me to elevate my vibrational level of energy to attract the matching vibrations of peace, abundance, success, self-love and more—all of which ancient and present-day research have tried to expose and make available to each one of us.

I have spent countless hours studying the wisdom of health experts and spiritual masters. I call it "gleaning from the experts," and as a result I have built a unique area of expertise myself, one that is far-reaching and covers a broad range of fields of study that reveal a better understanding of health, holistic well-being, the human experience, and the mysterious truth underlying mind, body, and spirit. I have come to know myself far beyond the layers of my skin right down to a cellular and quantum level to discover a power unlike anything I have ever known. The powerful, sacred, and beautiful treasures I have uncovered in my own expert field of study are yours to behold with me, and inscribed on every page of this book.

Powerful Knowledge

Max Planck, a theoretical physicist and Nobel Prize winner, shared this wisdom upon accepting his award, revealing critical and life-changing knowledge to us if we are willing to listen: "All matter originates and exists only by virtue of a force which brings the particle of an atom to vibration and holds this most minute solar system of the atom together. We must assume behind this force the existence of a conscious and intelligent mind. This mind is the matrix of all matter."

Planck studied the atom in depth, deeply enough to win a Nobel Prize, and he is trying to tell us something. Are you listening? He tells us that the conscious and intelligent force behind all existence is *us*—our thoughts, emotions, attitudes, ideas, beliefs, actions. This expert knowledge supports the truth about the great capacity we own to manifest the things we want to exist in our lives if we use the energy in our being and the world around us effectively.

Sparkling Insight

Our ways of living and being are the invisible forces that cause all of the elements of our lives to exist.

This one insight alone opens the door to so many more possibilities in life. We can't lose sight of the fact that we are the creators of the parts and pieces of our lives. Build your own wish list and be sure to include all of the intricate details so you can begin to intend each of them one by one into your beautiful life!

Some Expert and Master Levels of Knowing

The expert and master-level knowledge I share throughout the book along with the technologies and therapies I recommend all help you to activate your internal energy to connect with these magical forces surrounding you in every moment. These levels of vibration and experiences are available to anyone, but they are not found by those who do not seek the knowledge that contains them.

From the moment I became committed to study and learn the beautiful insights I share with you in this book, my life changed monumentally. It was my relentless commitment that created the spark that shone a light from one insight to the next and lit the path that led me to the secrets and miracles I create and experience daily. I have come to know energy in a very intimate way on a spiritual level, and I will share three sacred and beautiful experiences with you and some other magic and miracles along the way. I will continue to guide you first to understand energy the way I do so it doesn't seem like some fluff out of left field and so that you can easily understand and begin to experience living and being REAL Beautiful in your mind, body, and spirit as I have. If I can do it, you can too!

I do know that it is not because of the luck of the draw that I received these blessings in my life. Our innate being and the mystical elements of the life force inside and around us from moment to moment contain all the ingredients we need to make life all that we desire if we choose. Please do not be overwhelmed, as there is a lot of information and learning in this book. I designed it to be an in-house guru that you can turn to again and again. Please do not try to incorporate all of the knowledge, practices, and technologies all at once, but rather let yourself be guided to the information in the book that speaks to you first and then keep following as you will be led from one idea and practice to another in an order that works best for you. Please remember, because we are energy beings we require the taking in of energy and the letting go or releasing of it as well to be in our most optimal existence; one I know many of you have never known.

As we release or let go of energy, we can experience emotional or physiological effects. For example, you may have experienced the following:

- shedding tears as a release in your body and a way of healing grief or loss in life

- sweating as your body cleanses on a cellular level when you work out

- tiredness, headache, or nausea as your body detoxes from a raw diet, juicing, or a night on the town after too many glasses of red wine

If you can imagine yourself as a full glass of water, adding anything to the full glass will cause some of the contents to be displaced as the new contents take up space inside the glass. I have come to embrace the discomfort that some of these releasing experiences bring and recognize them as necessary to allow higher vibrational energy to replace the lower levels of energy inside my body.

I have heard many people relate that just after they start to take vitamins, they feel congested, as if they are getting a cold. It is really a sign of the antioxidants working through the body and bringing free radicals to the surface to be released. Many will stop taking the vitamins because they think the pills are not working, when in truth the vitamins are demonstrating that they do indeed work! Taking on one or two of the practices and applying them with consistency is what will reveal the magic inside the practice. Adding too many at once and not reaching any consistency with any of them gets you nowhere, or may be too overwhelming for your mind, body, and spirit to contain.

Sparkling Insight

Consistency is the staple ingredient you will need to add to any potion you choose to mix up from the insights in this book to make the magic behind every insight and practice unfold.

Energy-Raising Insights

I have always loved books that stretch my knowledge and bring new insights that require time and practice to assimilate into my knowing and being, and this book is no different. Transformation is impossible at the same level of knowing and being you live at in this moment. Stretch your limits and expand your horizons, so you can break down unwanted patterns and unblock the path to higher levels of vibrational energy that carry the miracles of life inside of you. Remember, as tough as this journey may seem, the technologies and insights I share have invisible helpers that come to your aid and get you through the necessary changes in some beautiful ways that you could never imagine.

Dr. David Hawkins

Energy expert Dr. David R. Hawkins reveals proof of the existence of an energy within us and one that surrounds us through his attractor research and a Map of Consciousness that calibrates the level of vibration from certain "processes of consciousness—emotions, perceptions, or attitudes, worldviews and spiritual beliefs" and could be extended to include all aspects of human behavior. This groundbreaking research, mostly hidden from the information streams well known to mass media, is not completely unknown.

I came to know Dr. Hawkins and his research through my lifetime spiritual master, Dr. Wayne Dyer, whose wisdom I am sharing as REAL Beautiful Gifts throughout the book. Dr. Hawkins reveals to us an understanding of the energy contained in our consciousness. His Map of Consciousness follows.

Adapted from the "Map of Consciousness" in Power vs. Force by Dr. David R. Hawkins

LEVEL	CALIBRATION	EMOTION
Shame	20	Humiliation
Guilt	30	Blame/Vindictiveness/Evil
Apathy	50	Despair
Grief	75	Regret
Fear	100	Anxiety
Courage	200	Affirmation
Neutrality	250	Trust
Willingness	310	Optimism/Hope
Acceptance	350	Forgiveness
Love	500	Reverence
Peace	600	Bliss
Enlightenment	700–1000	Ineffable

The higher the level of consciousness calibration, the more positive the attitudes/mind state, and thus the attraction of matching energy patterns will occur. In his book Power vs. Force, Dr. Hawkins tells us, "man is immobilized in his present condition by his alignment with enormously powerful attractor energy patterns which he himself unconsciously sets in motion." This statement and the calibration levels revealed in Dr. Hawkins' research remind us of the power we have to adjust our own energy to a higher calibration and that we are constantly attracting matching levels outside of us. This knowledge also reminds us of the power we own in knowing ourselves as an energy system. Once we have this knowledge, we become more motivated to watch over and do what is required to keep vibrating at the highest level possible. We all know what it is like to feel fear or anger, but I find it motivating to know that if I manipulate my energy levels through the practices and technologies related in this book, I can simply lift myself from these emotions and raise myself up to higher ones.

It is motivating to let go of fear and anger when there are ways to do this beyond talking ourselves out of these states. I find it interesting to know that fear and anger are energies that attract more of the same, and thus just by staying in these emotions we actually cause them to persist. If we make a conscious decision that we no longer want to have fear or anger as a part of our experience, we lift our consciousness and energy through certain activities, and we step out of fear and anger by our own choice. Lower levels of energy in and around us make us feel anxious, fearful, and depressed; higher levels make us feel, calm, peaceful, and happy. I call this truth *plain and simple science.*

Beyond the power of knowing that we can control and calibrate the energy levels we want to have in our bodies by managing them through technologies developed to raise them, we become even more powerful in knowing that once our own energy is uplifted, we can cause other people's to rise, in ways similar to Watson's Theory of Caring, a foundational model of care underpinning my Nursing practice, that incites the transferring of energies between us that can heal. The example below demonstrates how really powerful we are when we understand ourselves as an energy being.

According to Dr. Hawkins's research, one individual calibrating at Level 400 counterbalances 400,000 individuals below 200. This is captivating knowledge! When groups of meditators gather together and raise their level of vibration—meditation has been proven to do this—they create what is known as the Maharishi Effect. This rise in energy has the ability to influence the consciousness of people in the area of the meditators to such a degree as to cause a decrease in the crime rate and a rise in the stock market.

This research proves that we all have the power within us to heal the world as we calm and soothe it with the energies we choose to contain inside of us, and as we affect all things in our path, including ourselves.

Chapter 7

The Secret Wonders of Our Being

*What lies behind us and what lies before us
are tiny matters compared to what lies within us.*
—Ralph Waldo Emerson

The Miracles in Our Human Design

*A*s Emerson relates in the quote that opens this chapter, when we learn about the millions of brilliant interactions that take place inside our body and are unseen by the naked eye, we begin to realize the true miracle of our existence.

I think I became a believer in the impossible—in magic and miracles—on a deeper level when I witnessed and studied the inner workings of the human body. I saw the hidden and most beautiful secrets we take for granted and many of us never come to know. Unlocking the secrets inside you requires a willingness to study and learn more about who you really are. For those who refuse, the secrets remain locked inside and unusable.

The secrets behind who we are unfolded as I began to honor the brilliance of the physical, biological, physiological, emotional, mental, and spiritual parts of our being. In order for you to unlock the secrets I am talking about, you must be willing to take on a "new set of knowings," as Dr. Dyer advises in Gift #1. Let's learn more about the multiple aspects of our being so I can start sharing more secrets with you!

The Magic In and Around Us

I am very grateful for the opportunity to gain deeper perspectives and knowledge about how the body works, in a physical sense alone. My education in Nursing and the vast amount of health literature I have studied, both formally and informally, has played a large role in this cultivation. At the same time, even the education I have gained up to and including this moment only scrapes the surface of all there is to know and uncover about the mysteries and magic taking place in and around us from moment to moment.

I have been awed and astounded by the intricate, the delicate, the powerful, the divine, and the complicated truth behind our human existence, even at this superficial level. This minimal amount of knowing has made me realize how much I really don't know—yet at the same time, it opened the door to new understandings that have changed my view of who we are as human beings forever.

Being open to accept new knowledge and know there is so much more to know as I have stated before, is priceless wisdom. This practice and life principle that guides me has kept me humble and searching for deeper knowledge from experts and spiritual masters. As a result, I have been privileged to have secrets shared with me and doors opened to some of the wonders of living and being.

Powerful You

In the book *Your Hands Can Heal You: Pranic Healing Energy Remedies to Boost Vitality and Speed Recovery from Common Health Problems* by Stephen Co and Eric B. Robins, MD, with John Merryman, there is a revealing quote that reminds us again of the hidden powers inside of us that get overlooked because we can't see them— just because we can't see them doesn't mean they don't exist:

> Your body heals itself. … Through some process we don't fully understand, your body has the amazing, innate ability to repair itself. But medical science does not know how to do this, and it doesn't know what force powers the healing process. We know intuitively that there must be a consciousness behind this self-healing ability, one that knows how to work in the same way our body knows how to breathe without having to command our lungs to inhale and exhale.

One brilliant interactive anatomy course I took in university helped me to believe magic was possible after I saw many miracles taking place inside my body without my knowing. Like a humble philanthropist, it works faithfully and often without the gratitude and recognition it deserves.

Dr. Caroline Miller, editor of the American Board of Hypnotherapy and Dean of Academic Studies at the American Institute of Hypnotherapy and authors Frank Caprio, MD and Joseph R. Berger capture the truth in the revised version of the book *Healing Yourself with Self-Hypnosis* about the unyielding power of the human body. The following excerpt says it all:

> The complexities of the human mind are frequently talked about. However, much less attention is paid to the self-preserving and regenerating characteristics of the human body. Literally trillions of reactions take place every second within each bodily cell, making the body capable of actually renewing itself every five days, the skin replaces itself every month, the liver is replaced every three months. Every year, more than 95% of the atoms in our bodies are replaced with new ones. Every second or so, we inhale one set of gases, churn it through our entire system, and inhale a different set.
>
> Each of us has a bloodstream that contains 25 trillion red cells. It moves through approximately 60 thousand miles of blood vessels, regulating bodily temperature, sorting and carrying properly sorted hormones, enzymes, and nutrients to precisely the right location at exactly the right time. We know the neurons in the nervous system are the chemical

transmitters of messages from the brain to the body. Everything is controlled, from the heartbeat and motor abilities to sensory perceptions and emotional responses. Thoughts and emotions are transmitted to specialized areas of the brain, which in turn, sorts it all out with precision.

I love the brilliant knowledge in this excerpt because it helps us to appreciate the masterpiece the human body really is and the awe-inspiring interactions that take place from second to second automatically, faithfully, quietly, and unseen to the naked eye, behind the scenes of our lives.

As with an iceberg, what you see above the water is nothing compared to what lies beneath the sea or "see" level. Yet many will truly only know an iceberg from its above-water view, and have a similar lack of understanding of the full potential of the human mind, body, and spirit. Only the things that they can see become their truth and level of knowing about themselves and the world at large. As a result, many live and build the foundation of their lives upon only the things they can see, while others manifest and create lives solely based on the unseen.

Those who live from the uncovered truths decoded by many ancient and present-day spiritual masters, researchers, and experts know the magic I speak of because this is where the pathways to heaven on earth lie. These same people talk of magic and utopias that those who cannot feel or see call hocus pocus. They miss the opportunity to explore the depths of themselves and their world to behold the treasure that sits waiting to be opened on the road less traveled. To find the treasure requires some deep reflection and contemplation, an open mind, and adjusted eyesight. The seekers and searchers are rewarded with the mine of gold Rumi describes at the start of chapter 10. The lives and realities they build are full of possibilities and reflect their dreams while others spend a lifetime desiring but never find the things they wish for.

Knowing the regenerative, healing, and magnetic powers of the physical body requires one to look deeper into the science of the body and begin to unlock the sacred secrets it owns. It's clear to see the error in believing that this is all there is to you, me, and the iceberg. I choose to expect that there is so much more I don't know and to remain open to explore all that is beyond my limited human eyesight. When I use my third eye, or eye of insight that can be opened through the technologies I share with you, I am blessed to see all that is unseen to the naked eye. I have always chosen to view all things beneath the "see" level of the human eye and have experienced the magic and miracles that live and breathe at this often unexplored depth.

Heed the wisdom of these insightful words from Friedrich Nietzsche revealing the secrets some have found and others have not:

"And those who were seen dancing were thought to be insane by those who could not hear the music."

The Secrets That Surround You

What is an aurora borealis? Nothing but the sun's energy interacting with the earth's energy, producing heat that glows. *What is the sun?* Nothing but hydrogen atoms combining and releasing the energy of charged particles in the form of heat and light. *What is lightning?* Nothing but the energy in rain clouds interacting with the energy in the ground producing electrical sparks. And let's not forget the magical sparks that come to life or light in the darkness, when static electricity is made. They are all beautiful expressions of the magic power that shows up in the moments of our daily living.

So many of the things we find miraculous in our daily lives are simply expressions of the energy in and around us from moment to moment:

- the warm tingle felt from an act of human kindness
- the acceptance and peace felt from a genuine smile
- the awe of inhaling the fragrance of a simple flower in bloom
- the high felt from being in love
- the powerful rushing of water from a waterfall that illuminates our lives with electrical resources
- a healing song that inspires the soul
- the millions and trillions of electrical impulses that beat our hearts and assimilate the food and fluids we drink to feed mind, body, and spirit with this "life force" so powerful, it controls whether we live or die

The same energy force that runs through all of the miracles listed above is a part of you and every potential miracle that can be created by you. Pure and simple energy, all of it! I see the insights related above as sparks or glitter that light up and call out to us in our fast-paced lives to help us remember who we really are: energy beings. These are real and meaningful bits of knowledge that have the power to change your life. I am frustrated and challenged by the fact that this life-saving and transforming knowledge isn't more exposed, honored and revered in our Western societies. It remains mostly withheld from the general public and not on the agenda or a part of the ideals of governments and conglomerates. I do know why.

Chapter 8

Enlightened Master of Our Time: Donna Eden

Your body's energies are the most natural medicine that exists,
able to precisely orchestrate the body's self-healing
capacities wherever required.
—Donna Eden

Energy Medicine Secrets for Beauty, Power, and Healing

Speak to Your Body in a Language it Understands

*P*RESENT-DAY CONVENTIONAL MEDICINE ALREADY USES energy to observe illness inside our bodies through diagnostic tools like ultrasound (high-frequency sound waves or vibrations), PET (positive emission tomography) scans, MRI (magnetic resonance imaging), and CT (computed tomography) scans that measure the vibrational frequency of tissues to determine abnormal diseased cell growth. It seems logical to believe that as energy beings, we could manipulate the energy in our bodies to help heal ourselves as well. If we observe closely the healing of a simple cut on our own bodies, we witness again the invisible power of healing inside us that automatically takes over to protect us, and in time the wound disappears completely because of this magical and intangible force.

My own interest in the healing profession and countless hours of research and study to understand healing on multiple levels has enlightened me, and I have been intrigued by this invisible power inside of us. I have been equally interested in individuals who are trained and experts in the field of energy medicine.

In this chapter, I honor the life and work of clairvoyant, intuitive healer, and insightful master of our time Donna Eden. Her vast knowledge and experience in energy medicine makes her the most sought-after expert in this healing field. With an infectious spirit and undeniable light, she shines through the darkness to expose the truth behind our human design and the possibilities available to you and me that bring health and vibrancy to mind, body, and spirit.

From a young age, Donna was able to see the nine energy systems of the body:

- the meridians
- the chakras
- the aura
- the electrics
- the Celtic weave
- the five rhythms
- the triple warmer
- the radiant circuits
- the basic grid

According to Donna, the body consists of three types of energy: electrical energy (the energy stored and emitted in every cell of the body), electromagnetic energy (moving electrical energy), and subtle energy (energy undetected by measuring instruments, but with remarkable effects for those on the receiving end of energy healing treatments).

Donna suffered many health challenges that led her to seek further assistance from healing approaches outside conventional medicine, and to understand her body on a deeper level. She uncovered some of the secret energy and sacred science inside our bodies and beyond, and she healed herself from debilitating illnesses, such as hormonal imbalances, extreme metabolic issues, multiple sclerosis, hypoglycemia, a heart attack at twenty-seven years of age, the late onset of asthma in her thirties, and a malignant breast tumor at age thirty-four. Now she heals many around the world.

These powerful gems are only a small sampling of the many energy teachings Donna shares. To learn more about this amazing healer in action, please visit Donna's website at innersource.net. I urge you to view one of Donna's instructional DVDs to witness with your own eyes the powerful influence her energy techniques can have. It is truly magical to watch her balance and heal those who reach out to her.

In her search to understand health from the inside out, Donna generously ignites healing around the world. In my own search for effective knowledge to help guide women to understand themselves better as energy beings, I was drawn instinctively, intuitively, and synchronously to Donna's work, and our connection stands as one of the many consistent magical happenings I experienced as I wrote this book.

As you become more familiar with yourself as an energy being, practice the energy medicine techniques Donna has created to empower and heal women. Tap the acupressure points described with each healing exercise. Take note of how your body feels before and after you tap, massage, or trace.

Acupressure Points for Women

A few things to remember before you get started with these exercises from Donna Eden's book *Energy Medicine for Women*:

- *Strengthening points* are acupressure points that replenish depleted energies and strengthen energy meridians.

- *Sedating points* release blocked or excess energy to strengthen energy meridians.

- When you are guided to take a breath during the energy medicine practices, take a slow deep breath in for eleven seconds, hold for 11 seconds and then release for 11 seconds through the nose.

Three Thumps

Health Benefits:

- increases immunity

- protects the body from illness and disease

- increases vitality, improving a sense of well-being in the mind, body, and spirit

K-27

Beauty Gland

Spleen Acupuncture Points

Spleen Acupuncture Points

Spleen Neurolymphatic Reflex Points

Spleen Neurolymphatic Reflex Points

K-27, Beauty 'Thymus' Gland and Spleen Points for Three Thumps

1. *K-27 Point:*

   Sparkling Insight

   When tapped, K-27 influences all other energy meridians in the body.

   - Find and then palpate your right and left collarbone with your fingers, and then move your fingers along the collarbone toward the center of your body where the collarbone ends.

   - Once you have followed the collarbone with your fingertips inward to the end corners of each bone, drop your index and middle fingers on either side about one inch below this point and into the indentation or soft spot that exists there.

   - Begin firmly tapping or massaging these acupressure points as you take in a long and deep breath through your nose.

   - As you continue to tap/massage, hold the breath you have just taken in for eleven seconds and then slowly release the same breath as you continue to tap on the K-27 points.

   - Repeat your breathing/tapping/massaging sequence for three more breaths.

2. *Tarzan Thump*: This stimulates and resets the thymus gland—our "beauty gland" that gives us life through strong immunity and empowers the essence of who we are.

   - Trace your four fingers down 2 inches from K-27 across to the center of your chest or sternum.

   - Take the flat part of your four fingertips and tap firmly as you breathe in and out, as you did above for K-27, for 3 breaths.

3. *Spleen Points*: Tapping these points increases energy, balances blood sugar, and boosts immunity.

- Tap with fingers and thumb the spleen neurolymphatic reflex points that sit one rib under the center line of each breast.

- Tap with four fingers and thumb the spleen acupressure points on either side of the body that sit about 4 inches beneath the armpits.

- Breathe in and out three times as described above in the sequence for K-27.

Triple Warmer Smoothie

Triple warmer is one of the most potent energy systems in the body. It works in concert with the master gland of the body, the hypothalamus, which controls breathing, blood pressure, body temperature, heart rate, and hormone production. Triple warmer governs the adrenal glands and the production of cortisol and adrenaline. These vital hormones are released in response to any threat that comes our way to provide us with the energy we require to flee and move out of the way of danger. Unfortunately, the mounting stress in our Western society causes this "fight or flight" system to be activated too regularly, causing an overload of these chemicals in the body. That, in turn, begins to deplete our energy as it puts stress on multiple systems in the body—heart, muscles, blood vessels, stomach, liver, and so on.

Calming the triple warmer energy system with the powerful magnetic energy we own in our fingers to soothe the "fight or flight" response in the body is one of the simplest and most powerful ways to bring instant soothing and healing to mind, body, and spirit.

Health Benefits:

- calms our mind, body, and spirit so it can heal

- stabilizes our energy and keeps life force pulsing through us

- decreases the effects of stress in the body

- balances hormones

- strengthens immunity

A.   B.   C.

Triple Warmer Smoothie

1. Place and hold your four fingers from each hand side by side at your temples. Press and hold the fingers gently into the temples. As you do this, breathe in slowly and deeply through your nose, hold the breath for eleven seconds and then slowly release the breath through the nose. Don't forget to feel the warmth of the healing energy that will spread from the high dose of oxygen you give yourself in this breathing exercise while you tend to your overworked triple warmer energy system.

2. As you begin your second breathing sequence, slide and press your fingers to follow along the outside perimeter of the ear and then down the sides of your neck. Stop, press, and

breathe at each point along this path until you reach the place where your neck meets your shoulders.

3. Once your fingers reach the junction between the sides of the neck and the shoulders, allow your hands to settle, palms down, on your shoulders as you grab hold of each shoulder and create some pressure with your fingers along the back of your shoulder blade.

4. Continue with a new breath in through the nose as you slide your fingers across your shoulder blades down onto your chest in front of you. End with your palms flat on your chest and crossed over the center of your heart chakra (upper chest).

5. Hold this position as you complete three full breaths.

Triple Warmer Tap

Health Benefits:

- Calms our fears as it intercepts the fight or flight response in the body

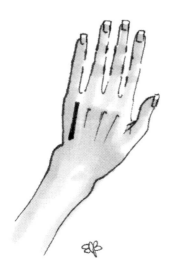

Triple Warmer Tap

The Triple Warmer Tap turns off the fear response in the body and stabilizes the life force that strengthens health and well-being. Fear depletes the life force within us.

1. Place your right or left hand palm down over your chest.

2. Tap with your other hand/fingers in the depression line between your pinkie finger and your ring finger away from the knuckle and toward the wrist.

3. Begin tapping as you complete the eleven-second breath sequence 3 times.

4. Repeat the sequence above for the other hand.

Spleen Meridian Flush and Tap

As Donna Eden explains in *Energy Medicine for Women,* "Spleen meridian is considered the 'mother' of all the body's energies." Its function is largely about keeping all systems functioning at their best. It governs our menstrual cycle, hormone balance, and metabolism. When we are stressed and fearful in life, we activate our triple warmer energy system, which steals energy from our spleen meridian. The spleen meridian loses its ability to protect us, and we gradually lose our health, strength, and spirit.

Health Benefits:
- strengthens the spleen meridian
- increases metabolism
- supports weight loss
- increases energy
- brings strength to the whole body
- controls menstrual blood flow
- brings balance to our hormones

- nurtures us in moments of stress
- strengthens the sex organs and uterus

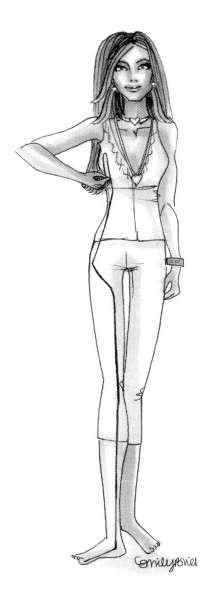

Spleen Meridian Flush and Tap

To perform the Spleen Meridian Flush and Tap, follow these steps:

1. Stand with hands flat open and at your side, with your fingers pointing down.

2. As you take a deep breath in through your nose, bring your hands up the sides of your body toward each armpit.

3. Breathe out slowly as you keep your hands flat and move them back down your sides to your waist.

4. When you reach your waist, cross your hands over the front of your hipbones and continue moving your open hands and palms down the inside of your legs, across your inner ankle bones, and up the inside length of your foot. Continue moving your hands along this path as your hands move out beyond your big toe.

5. Take another deep breath in through your nose before you retrace your actions backwards with your hands and palms open—big toe, inner ankle bone, trace inner legs up to hip bones and across to the side of your upper torso upward to just below the armpits. Release your breath slowly as you retrace the path upward from the toe three more times.

6. To end: tap the spleen neurolymphatic reflex points one rib below the midway point of each breast for 11 seconds as you complete 1 full breath sequence and then tap your spleen acupressure points on each side of your upper torso (four ribs down from the armpits) while you complete the eleven-second breath one more time.

Homolateral Crossover

In energy medicine, it is optimum to have the energy flow in the body crossing over in figure-eight patterns. When this crossover is not present, your energy is said to be in a *homolateral pattern.*

If you are depressed, chronically ill, or exhausted, your energy is not crossing over. To correct this, add the homolateral crossover technique below to your daily energy medicine routine.

Health Benefits:

- improves depression
- speeds healing
- restores energy balance in the body
- improves clarity and brain function.

Homolateral Crossover

1. Begin this technique by tapping K-27 (just about one inch below each clavicle in the indentation point described in the Three Thumps exercise). Tap firmly as you follow the breath sequence described at the start of this section on acupressure points.

2. Complete a full body stretch as you reach for the sky.

3. *Homolateral Crawl:* Start marching, lifting your right arm and right leg together and then your left arm and left leg together. (If this is difficult to do, your energy is already crossing over, which is a good sign). This is how you want your energy to be moving. If your energies are already crossing over, you can proceed to step six. If the homolateral crawl is easy for you, then your energies are moving homolaterally, which is not what you want. Complete 12 full homolateral march steps for each arm/leg raise and then move on to the crossover crawl in the next step.

4. *Crossover Crawl:* Keep marching, this time raising your right arm and left leg together and then your left arm and right leg for a count of twelve.

5. Switch back to the Homolateral Crawl for twelve counts and repeat this back-and-forth sequence between the Homolateral Crawl and the Crossover Crawl 3 more times. End this sequence with 12 more Crossover Crawls. Your energies are now crossing over.

6. Complete two more sets of 12 Crossover Crawls (step #4), and then tap/massage your K-27 point again to finish.

Energy is the living, vibrating ground of your being,
and it is your body's natural self-healing elixir,
its natural medicine.
—Donna Eden

Chapter 9

The Goddess Within

Do not use your energy to be perfect in body, but use your energy to find the perfection of who you truly are. You are the beauty of the universe.
—Mary Hunt

Shakti

*Shakti energy is a divine and sacred force that lives within us
that rises up in response to energy technologies and binds us
to the powerful, creative and magical pulse of the universe.*

Finding Shakti

ANCIENT SCIENTISTS AND PRESENT-DAY RESEARCHERS have revealed to us a mysterious and mystical energy that lives at the base of the spine and becomes activated when we apply specific practices and technologies. This energy is called *Shakti*. The essence of this intelligent energy, when awakened, brings forth the flow of our innate spirit to strengthen us and uncover the truth of our being. All you have to do is take action to call upon it. It is truly a magical experience. You begin to heal old hurts, experience new horizons, and know yourself more clearly as love and confidence abound. This mystical energy does it for you. All you have to do is be willing to do the things that ignite it.

When you connect to Shakti or this goddess that lives inside, you'll know it. You will enter a new world filled with light, love, healing, and possibilities, and you will begin to live at higher levels of being than you ever thought possible. You will feel carried and supported by an indescribable essence—but have no doubt of its power, for it will be one you have never known before. Your smile will widen and your gratitude will expand in response to the magical gifts Shakti offers.

Author and healer Maya Tiwari, in her book *The Path of Practice,* relates some of the wisdom and knowledge from her own Indian culture about the goddess that lives within us: "*Shakti* means the spirit of the primordial feminine energies within and its activity promotes the union of the mind, body, and spirit." Shakti power is a part of the highest power that runs the universe and shares this power with us. When my own Shakti became activated as a result of the powerful energy practices I share in this book, I was completely moved by the clarity and power I experienced. My insecurities seemed to melt away, and I saw my beauty—mind, body, and spirit—for the first time.

I wish for every woman to feel this power that eluded me for so long. I felt whole, connected, and on purpose, and these feelings enhanced my outer beauty as well. I felt beautiful and sacred in a way unlike anything I had ever known. I believe you have to experience it yourself to really know what I am talking about. If you sit in disbelief or know you haven't had this experience yet, keep reading!

The following exercises can cause your Shakti to stir and awaken. They are based in ancient wisdom not familiar to most of the Western world. I ask you to be open to insights outside your scope of knowledge and be willing to believe that there could be things you don't know, that you don't know.

Secret Ancient Sacred Healing for Women

All of the exercises below help to rebalance the hormones, rejuvenate the womb, and heal the female spirit.

Yoni Mudra I

This hand position opens the flow of life force or *prana* into the body and female organs to enhance the rhythm and balance that awakens Shakti inside the body.

1. Hold the palms of your hands facing up in front of your heart

chakra (at the center of your chest) while the edges along the pinkie fingers are lined up side by side.

2. Cross the right pinkie finger over the left.

3. Cross the ring finger on the right hand under the left ring and middle finger and let the left index finger grab and hug onto it.

4. Let the left ring finger slide naturally under the right ring finger and over the right middle finger. Once again, let the right index finger grab on to the left ring finger.

5. As you twist both hands in towards each other, allow your middle finger tips on both hands to meet and press together while the pinkie fingers curl to hold onto one another and the index fingers stay curled around the ring fingers. The thumbs will rest naturally side by side with the tips pointing up. It may take a couple of tries to bend your fingers into this position.

6. Once you manage the position, make sure your hands are at your heart chakra/center of chest and breathe in through your nose using the eleven–second breath: breathe in for 11 seconds, retain the breath without pressure for 11 seconds and then release the breath for 11 seconds.

7. Continue holding the *yoni mudra I* while you repeat the eleven-second breath for 11 minutes. Try to envision a red glowing light inside your root chakra/lower pelvic area.

Breath of Fire/Kapalabhati Breath

This breathing exercise is very good to do outside of menstruation to detox and nurture the womb. It balances and detoxes the mind, body, and spirit; brings power back to the lower chakras that house female organs; and rejuvenates and heals with life-force power.

1. Sit in a comfortable position as you keep your spine and neck straight. Breathe in and out quickly and deeply through the nose. At the same time, let your abdomen expand as you breathe in, and pull in towards the spine sharply as you breathe out.

2. Draw in breath and expel it quickly in this same manner for three minutes.

3. To end, take in a couple slow and deep breaths in and out through the nose.

Diamond Posture

The diamond posture is a great one for female organs, and it can be done while menstruating and as often as possible.

Healing Benefits:
- boosts immunity
- improves digestion
- strengthens confidence
- relieves negative energy from the body
- heals, strengthens, tones and brings balance to the lower body organs including the reproductive organs

1. While kneeling, sit on your heels and lower legs, with knees close together and heels under and embracing each side of your buttocks. Lower legs will be face down and pressing on the floor.

2. Breathe deeply into your lower abdomen from the level of the belly-button downward (involves the navel, sacral, and root chakras).

3. Hold this breath in without force for eleven seconds as you tighten your anal muscles and the muscles of the abdomen at the same time.

4. Release the breath through your nose and repeat the exercise for three or up to 11 minutes. Rest in diamond posture as often as you can.

I believe we are constantly living in a delicate balance between health and illness. We are healing parts and pieces of ourselves every moment of every day; just as we are quite able to cause injury or illness to our magnificent mind, body, and spirit, we can create healing and recovery as well. It is the unique and beautiful balance that can be created that brings forth the magic and mysteries inside our human design as it blends with the powerful essence of the universe. We need only be willing and conscious enough to know mind, body, and spirit intimately and energetically to receive the greater wisdom about the living and breathing magic that is a part of who we really are.

Chapter 10

Sacred Hidden Secrets

Why are you so enchanted by this world
when a mine of gold lies within you?
—*Rumi*

The Gold Inside You

*T*HE KNOWLEDGE I SHARE IN this chapter has been divinely downloaded to me. Higher insights like these are one of the many gifts given to us when we raise the vibrational energy inside our physical bodies. We become connected to an intelligence that is divine in nature for it is contained inside the higher streams of energy we all have access to. Like the breaking of a secret code, a clear understanding of the mysteries of life is revealed. I call these crystal clear insights sparkling jewels because they remove doubt, restore faith, inspire, inform, and carry us more wisely through the moments of our lives. It is the most exciting and magical thing when the insight is imparted. Those of you who have experienced it know what I am talking about. Like entering a secret library, the truth is found written on the pages of every sacred book found there. Because I am a believer that the right information comes to us when we are ready to receive it —and that there is always more to know— I humbly share the sacred ideas that follow with the greatest honor and reverence for God, the highest power in the universe that you and I are a part of. I am aware that these insights are only a small portion of the infinite number of secrets and amount of knowledge yet to be uncovered.

I have come to know some of the powerful secrets, or the "gold" Rumi speaks of in the transcendent quote that opens this chapter. He reminds us, like the secret messages that surround us, to stop searching for the gold (or beauty, power, healing, peace, love, happiness, success, abundance, prosperity, and so on) outside of us, for it lies within. The gold Rumi speaks of is part of the magic and miracles you will come to know in greater depth because of the hidden and sacred science I share with you in this book.

When I was just a little girl, I remember pretending I could perform magic and miracles like Samantha on the television show *Bewitched*. All she had to do was twitch her nose or snap her fingers, and instantly she got what she wanted or made events change to suit her every whim. I even loved to play for hours outside on the grass hills behind my house with my magic wand in hand, for it gave me the power and protection I seemed to be searching for even back then. When *Star Wars* hit movie screens, I wanted to contain "the force" that Jedi master Obi-Wan Kenobi taught Luke Skywalker. And what about Harry Potter, Hermione, and all the Hogwarts students? They were born with magical powers! Why couldn't I perform magic too? Even a recent trip to Disney World's Magic Kingdom reminded me of how we are whimsically called to believe in magic, superpowers, utopias, fantasy lands, castles, and happy endings in the world around us.

Right Before Our Eyes

If we look closely enough, the messages are all right in front of us. The idea of magic existing in life has followed me since I was young and as you can see in this book, the concept has stuck with me throughout my life. It has been a lifetime of musing, my intense study and research for the content of this book, my willingness to believe, and the countless miraculous events that have taken place while writing *(sage-like knowing, ongoing synchronistic events, a near-death experience, a heightened ability to communicate with those who have passed on, abundance on all levels flowing to me, thoughts turning into things before my eyes, healing moments, flickering lights, sacred sounds vibrating inside me, necessary information being revealed to me, asking and receiving, magical roses—I could go on, but that would be another book in itself)* that have become further evidence to me that we really do own magical powers. Because of the life-time connection and inspired interest I have been divinely given regarding the existence of magic and miracles, I believe part of my purpose is to help you to know this experience in your own life too!

I have broken the code and unlocked some secrets that are available to you as well if the pure and honest desire to seek and know their essence is inside your heart. You must see things in a new light. These countless and beautiful secrets are revealed when you understand the spirit or invisible part of you that Dr. Dyer describes below. All too often, people ignore this part of who they are. Dr. Dyer reminds us that even revered scientific minds have been mesmerized by this unseen deity that is housed within our physical body. It has the capacity to exist beyond physical death and influence matter, and the thoughts that are chanted in the mind outside of it resonate with a vibration that becomes the mastermind behind all that is created in one's life.

REAL Beautiful Gift #4
Insights from *Real Magic* by Dr. Wayne Dyer

"You have the capacity to create miracles and live a life of real magic, by using your invisible self to influence your physical reality. When you truly become a spiritual being first and a physical being second, and know how to live and breathe in this new alignment, you will become your own miracle worker."

Finding the Real You

Your spiritual being is the real you, secretly hidden inside the masterful interior depths of your physical body and mind. You are a miracle-making machine with superpowers that sit and wait to be uncovered and discovered. To unleash these powers you have to be willing to connect to the higher vibrations that contain them. There is a sacred path to this unbelievable power if we are willing to understand it. Call it God, divine intelligence, the source, magic and miracles, or whatever you please, for the name does not change its undeniable presence. And like the law of gravity rules the earth, this indescribable essence rules the universe, whether you choose to believe in it or not. I call this highest energy or power God. You decide what you will name it (divine mind, universal force, vital force, higher power and so on). To find it, you must seek to understand yourself and this highest power better—the two most misunderstood energy beings of all time.

The energy of this greatest power rules the universe. The energy of the spirit inside of you determines whether you know and understand this energy so that you can become one with it. When you connect to it, you will become powerful beyond your imagination.

The Secrets You Know Already

I have guided you so far to look inside the brilliant plasticity of the mind, the miraculous sagacity of the physical body, and the humbling intelligence in the world that surrounds you at any moment. All of it is simply energy. I showed you this so that you can see that you are the architect behind it all. The thoughts, beliefs, and ways of living and being you own and choose fill your being on a cellular level and radiate a frequency that pulls toward it and your physical being all matching frequencies. The energy you store inside your body becomes the raw material from which you build your life. Reflect on the energy you have created inside your body. Tabulate the sum of all of it—thoughts, beliefs, feelings, behaviors, emotions—and then decide whether you are building the life of your dreams or the life of your limited beliefs and fears.

Learning what thoughts, ideas, beliefs, emotions, habits, behaviors, and so on have the highest frequencies for connecting with the positive goodness life can bring—beauty, power, healing, love, peace, bliss, enlightenment, inspired purpose, success, abundance, prosperity, all the things that make us feel like magic is taking place—in some depth, is required. You already know you are an energy being. You will become the witness of the level of energy these things hold by observing what they bring into your life.

The Spirit Part of You

Sparkling Insight

Scientific research, sacred texts, and hidden secrets reveal the ways to raise the vibration of your energy being to the levels that connect to your higher self—that is, the spirit part of you—to make these positive opportunities possible. You have to believe first that you are the builder, not the tenant, of your mind, body, and spirit, so you can begin to ignite the REAL beauty inside you. This knowledge will help you come to know your spirit being that has direct access to the highest power we are seeking to find in this book, for it is the most powerful, beautiful, and fun part of who you are. Your spirit is the doorway to the highest consciousness and power in the universe.

When our spirit being is activated with our mind and body, magic and miracles happen. You have to be willing to get sacred with me in order to uncover the secrets inside you at greater depth. I believe the insights shared in the Bible, and other ancient and holy texts hold the sacred science we must learn to know the spirit part of who we are, just as we might study physiology and anatomy to know the inner workings of the physical mind and body.

Finding Spirit

Spirit is an essence or entity that is not visible to the naked eye, but clearly felt and known by the third eye and the energy centers within us. The American Heritage Dictionary defines it as "the vital principle or animating force within living beings."

I believe spirit to be the higher self or divine self that becomes known when higher vibrational levels of energy within the body and around it are activated. When this part of us is reached at these elevated levels, the highest truths, secrets, mysteries of life, and pathways to all that is good—beauty, power, healing, magic, miracles, kingdoms, heaven, sanctuaries—open up to us. This all happens because of our connection to this highest power or energy that rules over us. We can't reach our spirit being or the power of this great force without elevating the energy in our physical bodies to reach *spirit* levels.

The Secret Messages in Sacred Texts

The language of the Bible has always seemed like Shakespeare to me—and as I have found out in my study and research, it has felt just as ambiguous to many spiritual scholars as well. I have often asked in prayer for a clearer understanding. It is my curiosity, the mystery, and the confusion that have caused me to look further into the teachings of many sacred scriptures and from as many spiritual masters. I share my own interpretation of each spiritual quote related in this chapter based on the divinely guided insight I have been provided.

While growing up in a Catholic family, I was exposed to the Holy Bible and recall the stories in it about the miracles Jesus performed when he walked on water and healed the sick just by walking by them. I also remember this quote from John 14:12:

> *"Very truly I tell you, whoever believes in me will do the works I have been doing, and they will do even greater things than these, because I am going to the Father."*

My Interpretation...

When you believe in the things Jesus teaches *[love, faith, kindness, principled living containing higher vibrations and so on]* and apply them to your life, you will activate your spirit energy that is connected to God energy (the highest power in the universe), similar to that Jesus owned. It is the ways of living and being that Jesus, one of the greatest spiritual teachers on earth, guides us to that allows the flow of this magical and powerful field of energy to saturate our being and render us more powerful than we ever knew possible. When this energy flows through us we are able to achieve greater things than we ever thought possible.

Sparkling Insight

Thirteenth century poet and mystic Rumi reminds us in the following quote that in order to make better sense of our living and being we must search for truth from the inside by knowing ourselves as energy beings so we can open the door to the magic that is available to us. "I have lived on the lip of insanity, wanting to know reasons, knocking on a door. It opens. I've been knocking from the inside." We continue to be told to look inside ourselves!

Once again, we need to adjust our eyesight to witness the evidence that magical powers are within and around us! We hear of miracle workers, experience miracles ourselves, and speak of miraculous events, but often disregard them as coincidences, accidents or simple occasional unexplainable events. There are unbelievable things happening in and around us at great frequencies in every moment, if we really care to record them. Why is it that we seem almost afraid to believe that there might be miracles or that we might be miracle-makers? Is it mainstream media and social learning that have us so convinced we are not capable of more? They want us weak and dependent on their services and products, even medicated, so we miss the cues and signs leading us to the truth. Look at the countless number of healers and mediums in and around us, the equal number of miraculous healings that take place across the world, the brilliant insights uncovered by spiritual and enlightened masters, researchers and Nobel Prize winners, the unsung heroes in all of us who have been broken by tragedy and loss, yet like the sun, rise again to face another day. Where do these miracle wisdoms and abilities come from? And let us not forget the awe-inspiring flight of a bird, the blossom of a rose, the mystical whispers in the wind and the messages in the water...I could go on. These are just a small glimpse of the many miracles taking place in our everyday moments of living and being.

To help us understand better this "magical power" possibility, I turn to the gnostic gospel of St. Thomas, as it is known to reveal the hidden secrets behind the figurative words of Jesus. The quotes below are from *The Gospel of St. Thomas: The Hidden Sayings of Jesus* by Marvin Meyer and the New Revised Standard Version of the Bible. I have placed my own interpretation underneath each quotation.

If you do not fast from this world, you will not find the kingdom.
—Gospel of St. Thomas

My Interpretation...

If we don't step away from the world we live in outside of us that hides the knowledge (through mass media and social learning) we miss the opportunity to live the life of our dreams (that is, enter the kingdom/know the magic).

The kingdom of heaven is like treasure hidden in a field,
which someone found and hid; then in his joy
goes and sells all that he has and buys that field.
—Mathew 13:44

My Interpretation...

Some who find out about the hidden secrets experience the power/the magic/the kingdom and try to hide it from others for fear there will be none left for them, or out of fear that another might surpass their own power. This field of energy is secret because we have not been taught in our present-day society to understand the science behind our physical bodies as energy beings. I believe the power obtained from this mystical field of energy caused the ancient elite to hide this knowledge in the past and is the reason why it is still hidden in our own society today by conglomerates and advertisers. They fear that we might be able to heal ourselves and bring forth our own physical, mental, and spiritual beauty along with a life filled with beautiful miracles because of the knowledge we gain from the energy contained within our own human design.

Sparkling Insight

The real secret behind all of this power is in the sharing of it; in doing so we cause our own energy vibration to rise.

A Veil of Secrecy

Through the ages, individuals have kept this powerful information hidden for other reasons as well. Although ancient sage Hermes Trismegistus wanted others to be enlightened by the secret power I am guiding you to, he was inhibited. He taught hermeticism—mystical and alchemical writings that came from the first three centuries after Jesus died—in secret underground societies, always verbally and never written for fear of death if higher authorities found out that it was being shared. The beloved Yogi Bhajan, whose wildly powerful insights and Kundalini Yoga technology I am blessed to share later in this book, risked his life when he came from the East to the West to teach a secret and powerful science that allows us to enter the heaven on earth we seek. These true stories related throughout history can help us to understand the reason secrecy and fear still surround this enlightened knowledge and help us feel braver to step into our power. Let us not forget that we have also been taught that it is taboo or witchery, instead of sacred and beautiful. These negative labels have kept many of us away from the knowledge for fear of judgment or even worse, death if we admit to practicing or knowing the sacred truths.

And God's kingdom is inside you and outside of you.
Whoever knows oneself will find this. And when you know yourselves
you will know you are children of the living father.
—Gospel of St. Thomas

My Interpretation...

Once again, we are told the energy of this highest source of power lives inside and around us. When you realize this you will be astounded and you will create heaven on earth with this power. Knowing yourself as an energy being and learning how to raise the vibrational energy inside your physical body elevates you to the higher power or father of all energy. As related before, there are specific ways of living and being that uplift your vibration to higher levels where you meet up with this mysterious field of energy and allow it to live inside you. All of these heavenly frequencies can only be reached if we look inward to the secrets, sanctuary and sacred gifts woven inside the fabric of our own masterful and beautiful physiology. To say that we are *children of the living father* or God, is to say we are a part of this all-powerful energy source just like we share features similar to our own biological parents. If we are considered children of this highest power/God the Father, then we are made from or of it too, thus owning the same power and capabilities. We are afraid we will be called sinners or judged because the teachings in holy books have been misinterpreted and keep us from the truth of the real power we can have access to in our lives. We are the ones who choose whether we activate and use this power if we apply the insights and sacred practices I share in this book. It is that simple.

REAL Beautiful Gift #5
Insights from *Real Magic* by Dr. Wayne Dyer

"There are many things that you can do on a daily basis to bring out the 'Eden' that is your birthright. But whatever it is that you find yourself doing in the physical world, you must know that it is all driven by the divine invisible soul that has temporarily settled itself in your body."

Finding the Highest Power

Ask, and it will be given you; search and you will find;
knock and the door will be opened for you.
—Mathew 7:7

Let the one who seeks not stop until one finds. When one finds, he will be
astonished. One will reign, and having reigned, one will rest.
—Gospel of St. Thomas

My Interpretation...

If you haven't found the truth of your being, do not give up seeking it. Finding the truth requires search and study from knowledge less visible, more scientific and sacred than mainstream mass media, classroom textbooks and other social learning teachings.

Sparkling Insight

Let self-knowledge be at the top of your 'to do' list. If you seek the truth of your being with all your heart, an open mind, and genuine and revered effort, you will be guided to the truth of it and you will be astounded by the secrets, gifts, power, and treasures that are at your disposal. You will know your highest self and come face to face with this highest power that rules the universe.

We come to know of this miraculous power through searching the hidden messages in sacred texts written and preserved over thousands of years, whose clarity and understanding are revealed like a secret code that has been broken when we are willing to look outside the box into deeper and more sacred knowledge with a humbled heart. There are many who are unconscious and still don't know this power exists. There are some who are afraid of it, some who are afraid to share it and even more who cannot humble themselves enough to embrace it. This power rules us whether we know about it or care to seek it, or not. It is only when we know and honor its presence that the door is opened. Just like magic, we are enlightened and finally get it. As though invisible ink was losing its power, the sacred secrets reveal themselves to us. I love it when this information is mystically handed to me. I get an excited warm chill inside my body that reminds me that I have made contact with this sacred field or power and that I am holding a magic wand in my hand. Holding and activating the magic wand is empowering and exhilarating at the same time. I call this experience '*simple, sacred, fun*'.

Jesus himself speaks of the mystery behind the teachings we look to guide us in Luke 8:10 when he reminds his own disciples "To you it has been given to know the secrets of the kingdom of God." He gives the clearest understanding of his teachings to his disciples so that they could help to bring clarity to his words and so understanding could be passed on to others through them over time.

These teachings are as old as the wisdom within them. Those who have connected to their own spirit within know the magical force I speak of. Ironically, we search and search to find the heaven we seek on earth, and it is hidden in the secrets inside our own physiology. Our energy vibration can be altered through specific ways of living and being, as Jesus and many spiritual masters try to teach us. They are all leading us to beauty, power, healing, bliss, peace, enlightenment, success, abundance, and so on; the magic and miracles of life! When you have these things you have "entered the kingdom" related throughout sacred texts.

Interestingly enough, the guidance we have been given in holy books to love one another and ourselves in order to feel peace and joy reflect the findings in the spiritual research performed by Dr. Hawkins, as mentioned in chapter 6. "Love" calibrates on higher levels within the map of consciousness, as do courage, willingness, joy, peace, and enlightenment, while states of awareness like guilt, fear, and anger calibrate lower. Could it be that Jesus was trying to tell us to love ourselves and others, be not afraid, and heal our anger so that we could raise the vibrational levels of energy inside our bodies to create the sanctuaries and paradises that make us feel that we are the royal ones living in the kingdom or palace? Let us remember Dr. Hawkins' research related in chapter 6 expressing the higher calibrations found when our ways of living and being contain the vibration of love, peace, and kindness. These are the ways of living and being that the greatest avatars, saints and spiritual masters of time try to guide us to as well. They are guiding us to the ways of living and being that raise our vibrational energy. In doing this, they are giving us the keys to the kingdom!

I am convinced of these sacred insights and this research because every time I am able to choose love over any other choice, I find my physical body overcome by an inner waterfall that fills me with an elixir that makes me feel high and capable of creating miracles in life.

Gems, Jewels, and Rubies

The *Shabd Guru,* sacred hymns or *shabds* imbued with the spiritual insight of ten gurus and other spiritual masters contain some very secret and sacred power. *Shabd*—the sound current that cuts the ego—written from the Gurmukhi alphabet and containing *Gurbani* (a sacred language of enlightened words contained within the Shabd Guru). The word *guru* is defined as the teacher or knowledge that transforms darkness into light. The Shabd Guru own musical scores that contain the rhythm and sound that is scientifically orchestrated and played out in the pattern the tongue makes with the reflexes on the upper pallet of the mouth (secret pressure points). This pattern activates neuroendocrine responses in the body that help heal and bring balance to the mind, body, and spirit as it connects us to our higher self and the highest power in the universe.

The *Japji Sahib* is a *shabd* within this holy book. I felt connected and guided to the sixth *pauri* in this shabd as I wrote this chapter. I have had many secrets revealed to me in my reflection on these teachings, and all the sacred texts I have researched and studied before and during the writing of this book. I have found the sacred gifts related in a line within the sixth *pauri*: "One will find in his mind gems, jewels and rubies, if he were to act upon and listen to the instructions of the guru."

Sparkling Insight

The gems, jewels, and rubies are the gifts we receive or the gold Rumi speaks of when we reach higher levels of vibration through the sacred science being revealed in the insights, technologies and energy practices that can transform us on a cellular, chemical and energetic level—and in turn lead us to the kingdom of heaven referred to in holy books.

Darkness Turns into Light

The higher insights imparted to me while connected to higher vibrations in my search to understand heaven, life and miracles tell me that heaven is not a place, but a realm or sacred field of energy we can connect with to find higher knowledge and the beautiful gifts I have described as gems, jewels, magic, and miracles— along with heavenly connections to loved ones who have transitioned from the physical world. I believe that the highest power I speak of is not a religion or a man in the sky, but an all-knowing, divine and intelligent energy that rules the universe and all that is created with a power so great that if you don't understand it, you can create suffering and havoc in your life and never know you are the cause of it. I came to know these things and the spirit part of me when I understood myself as an energy being. I know now that I am the creator of my energy vibration level as a result of the levels of energy I allow to penetrate my being, whether in my thoughts, beliefs, feelings, emotions, behaviors, actions, or the ways of living and being I choose. These are the ways to my spirit self and they open the door to this indescribable and unseen power that brings forth all the beauty, power, healing, abundances, and intentions we ask for from our hearts. These are the beautiful secret insights being shared with us in sacred texts and taught by spiritual masters over time.

Jesus, his disciples, and many spiritual masters and religions and their followers have all attempted to help us understand and know our spirit and the connection to this energy source, but many have been confused or misguided because of the mystery behind the meaning or translations of these teachings. Call this power God, a divine source, a universal mind, a sacred field of energy—it is all the same power and deserves our honor and reverence.

When you know it and understand it, you connect to the invisible greatness inside you and thus hold a magic wand, lightsaber, or royal scepter in your hands.

The next two chapters are really extensions of this one, for they touch on the magic that is possible when we come to know ourselves as energy beings, as revealed before and within this chapter. In chapter 11, I share three of the many beautiful connections I have made with loved ones in heaven, one of which includes a walk inside the doors of heaven through my own near-death experience. When you uplift your vibrational energy to connect with your own spirit— that is, the real you—you open the door to your connection with this reigning power that oversees all creation in your life and in mine.

In chapter 12, I expose the sacred and hidden teachings of Gregg Braden, the third enlightened master of our time I share with you in this book. Gregg brings light to the deeper levels of miracles, beauty, and the power we own inside of us to become the designers of our own lives by adjusting our thoughts, feelings, and emotions. Gregg's research and study of lost, hidden, and sacred texts in remote lands help us see more clearly the magic power we own.

REAL Beautiful Gift #6
Insights from *Real Magic* by Dr. Wayne Dyer

"It dwells within you, in that invisible part of yourself, where the rules that pertain to the physical world simply do not apply. In your soul, your spirit or higher self, your mind or thoughts or whatever you choose to call it, lies the entryway to the world of real magic."

Chapter 11

Finding Heaven

What if you slept? And what if in your sleep you dreamed?
And what if in your dream you went to heaven,
and there plucked a strange and beautiful flower?
And what if when you woke, you had the flower in your hand?
—Samuel Taylor Coleridge

Flowers from Heaven

I OPEN THIS SPECIAL CHAPTER WITH a quote that appears in the front pages of Dr. Wayne Dyer's *Real Magic: Creating Miracles in Everyday Life* because it fully expresses the moments I have experienced in finding heaven in my life. Beyond the magic and miracles that pour into my daily living, I have been blessed to connect with loved ones who have passed on to the other side. The ability I have to make these connections helps me to experience heaven on earth in a different way. These connections happen because of higher levels of vibrational energy in the cells of my body—which I consciously uplift with all the approaches I share with you in this book. They open the doors to heaven for me. I believe we all have this ability.

As related in the previous chapter, there are many secret powers we own when we seek to understand them, believe in them in our hearts, and use the practices and technologies—the ways of living and being—that magnetically and energetically bring heaven to us. This realm not only connects us to our own spirit and the highest divine field of energy, it connects us to the spirit of those who have passed from this physical world.

From the first moment I read the words of Samuel Taylor Coleridge in Dr. Dyer's book, they spoke volumes to me, as they captured the truth of some powerful connections I have had with the "other side" and of the strange and beautiful flowers I have brought back from my visits to heaven while still on earth. My role as a caretaker at the doorway between life and death causes me to reflect and seek to understand this unchangeable aspect of life for us all. My dedicated and relentless search to understand heaven, where my own mother lives along with the countless patients who died as I stood with them at their bedside, affords me the privilege to uncover the secrets behind this mystery of life. As we learned in the previous chapter, when we seek with our whole heart, we find. This insight has comforted me in dealing with the loss of my mother and other loved ones.

Amidst the ongoing connections to my mother and other individuals from the other side for over twenty-five years, I have felt the energy of love, comfort, bliss, and spirit, and I have received divine guidance and healing when contact with this beautiful realm was made. The intensity and frequency of my union has greatly increased during the writing of this book, which becomes further proof to me without a doubt, it is the application of the insightful knowledge I include on these pages that has caused this. As I add this sentence to the book, my spirit lamp, as I now refer to it, continues to turn on several times a day. I know this is another message from loved ones who have passed, letting me know that they are with me and my family. This light began to turn on daily the week before I moved into my new house and has not stopped since. This is just another example of the little miracles and glimpses of heaven that saturate my day and continue to bring comfort, healing, and new insights to guide me further to uncover more beautiful secrets unknown in this moment.

Below, I share three real-life stories from my heart, revealing my connection to heaven. The final story includes a near-death experience that took me inside the doors of heaven. Before you read these stories, adjust your eyesight, as you would do to uncover the picture behind a "magic eye" photo. When we see with our third eye, stepping away from this physical world and tuning in to the world of energy that shows us clearer pictures of things as it uncovers the secrets of our power, we open the door to the unseen and those things unknown to us in the present moment. If you cannot learn to see with this new eyesight, you will not enter the world of possibilities that unfold when you do. This requires a change in belief that all the things I speak about are possible instead of impossible.

REAL Beautiful Gift #7
Insights from *Real Magic* by Dr. Wayne Dyer

"Be a willing student. Your level of readiness to grow and become your own miracle worker is simply a state of mind."

Messages from Heaven

A Mother's Voice

I had a dream about my mother just before the one-year anniversary of her death. When I woke from this dream, I felt like I had been with her all night long. In this dream, my mother hugged me and told me she loved me. She let me know that she was doing fine and that she was proud of me. These words answered every question that I had asked over and over in my mind since her death. When I awoke from the dream, I felt lighter as the pain of my grief lifted and a sense of comfort and peace over my mom's death penetrated. It was as if acceptance flooded my being. Even my sisters could sense the change.

Maybe you have had this happen to you as well when a sense of 'knowing" takes over? I couldn't really explain it at the time, but my mother was with me. I could feel her, hear her, and see her (with new eyesight) as I continued to listen to her gentle and loving guidance for many years beyond this dream. I was bringing home the strange and beautiful flower Coleridge refers to. The "beautiful flower" was the gift I had been given to have special access to heaven from earth, allowing me a new relationship with my mother beyond her physical death. Healed and renewed because of these heavenly moments, I moved forward in life with eyes open to this new reality. My new awareness kept the doorway open for my mother and I to walk through and continue our relationship as mother and daughter.

The poem below flowed effortlessly out of me onto paper after the dream about my mother. It wasn't until years later, when I removed it from the hidden pages of my Bible, that I realized every verse in the poem followed the progression of stages one passes through while grieving the loss of a loved one—denial, anger, bargaining, depression, and acceptance. It is normal to oscillate back and forth between these stages before coming to acceptance.

Dear Mom

Where are you now? I often cried.
I want you here beside me.   *[Denial and Bargaining]*
I want to see your pretty eyes. I want to see you smile.
I want to hear you talk to me,
You haven't for a while.

The endless tears I hide inside   *[Anger*
feel like they'll never end;   *Depression*
If only for one moment   *Bargaining]*
I could have you here again.

But through the darkness was a light
That with my memories hold,   *[Acceptance]*
I thought I felt you with me and my heart was not so cold.

So, Mother, if you hear me,
Please help me understand,
For now I go on living,
Until we meet again.   *[Acceptance]*

The Other Side

I lost my mother to the "other side" when I was twenty-five years old. Like many of you who have suffered such a loss, I began to question living, life, aliveness, and death, and I became very confused and a little overwhelmed by it all in some moments. The world as I knew it no longer made sense to me. In my deepest of sorrows, I remember begging my mother—wherever she was—and God—whoever he was—to please help me understand this loss and to lift me from the great darkness I was experiencing.

A couple of weeks before my mother died on Easter Sunday, March 26, 1989, I sat beside her as she lay in bed. She had been diagnosed with cancer over a year earlier and had been through a living hell in which she was lucky to have one day a month were she felt like a normal human being because of a chemotherapy regimen that took away much of her quality of life. Because I was a nurse and a caregiver to cancer patients, I knew all too well the telltale signs of a life that was slipping away. My mother held my hand after I gave her a shot of morphine to ease her pain and said, "I feel like I have disappointed you all, but I can't do this anymore!"

I was saddened at the meaning behind these words. With all that she had been through, how could she for one moment think she wasn't doing "good enough" living with cancer? Her words also signaled a transition through her stages of death, which I had witnessed before in my own nursing experience. I knew she was not to be too much longer in this physical world.

I hugged my mother tight and told her I was proud of all of her strength throughout this illness and that I couldn't have survived all that she had been through. She looked at me like a child, our roles reversed, and searched for my praise and then approval to let go. I told my mother that if she felt she couldn't do this anymore, I completely understood. My mother rose up from her bed and took her Bible from the nearby dresser into her hands. She gently searched through the pages and then handed me what I now call my "miracle prayer": the Novena of the Rose by St. Therese. She placed her Bible down and lifted a potted plant off the same dresser and handed it to me and said, "I want you to have this."

I gathered the final gifts she gave me together as I left her that day, knowing there was a reason behind them. My mother told me she was not afraid to die, only that she would miss me. Mystically, it is these gifts—the prayer card and the plant—she gave me that day, the day of her death (Easter Sunday), and the fact that she left this world with a sense of not being "good enough," that became the tools she uses to reach me and guide me from the other side. Her Easter Sunday transition from life guided me to notice the little bunnies that magically showed up in unexpected moments with a clear message from her saying, *I am here with you*. It is the uncanny ongoing delivery of roses in response to the novena that keeps me believing in magic, unseen forces, energy, and heaven on earth.

I've transplanted and shared the plant my mother gave me over and over with family, and I partake of the messages the plant sends me directly from my mother. When it is full of blossoms, I am growing too; when it has discolored leaves and dry soil, it reminds I need to take better care of myself. A little over two years ago, when my plant was threatened by a virus, my own life was equally threatened by pneumonia that brought me to the near-death experience I share in this chapter. The cleansing of the infected soil right down to the plant's fragile roots reflected the knowing I had that my pneumonia was cleansing me from a cellular level, washing away the lack of self-love and feelings of not being "good enough" that had been vibrating inside me for many years.

The plant continues to be one of the ways my mother communicates with me from heaven. I never dream about my mother anymore, but she connects with me outside of my dreams through the plant, bunnies, magical roses, music, people I meet, and most recently, my spirit lamp. I continue to communicate with my mother in the language we have somehow decoded together. Our connections can carry emotionally charged messages that stop me in my tracks, sparkle gently in my heart, or send waves of quiet comfort. One way or the other, the feeling and experience always stands out from everyday moments as a divine connection.

⌁

A Message from Jenna Glow

My palliative care nursing experience was the most beautiful mind-bending journey in all of my time spent nursing inside a hospital. It was equal in some ways to my training in maternity nursing, where I watched life begin. The miracle of new life left me intrigued, as did the mystery of death. I have been honored to be with those in my care as they transformed from physical being into the fullness of spirit.

Jenna Glow was a patient many nurses might have felt burdened by because of their heavy workloads. She was considered demanding in a sense, because she asked for help to get her makeup on and have her hair done. That little touch of color in her cheeks and lips made her feel better, I could tell. I knew I would request the same if I was in her position, so I never minded helping her complete these daily tasks. I knew it was her fear of all the transitions through the stages of dying that caused her to ring her call bell frequently.

It was true, Jenna was dying. It was this truth that gave me the energy to give her, just like every other dying patient, the little things she needed to allow her some sense of peace and comfort. I was trained to know I couldn't change the fact that my patients would die, but I could be the one to lessen their pain in the moments they had left on earth. Jenna and I developed a close relationship, and I knew she found solace in my presence.

On one particular day while caring for Jenna, I felt her watching me more intensely than usual. I even felt a little scared to restart her intravenous line that day, as her watchful eye made me feel a little unnerved. I intuitively picked up on some of the thoughts that were running through her mind. I had become fairly adept at reading energy and minds, although I never really trusted my ability until it was placed in black and white before my eyes. I have come to trust in this ability more over the years.

It wasn't until I was nearing the end of my twelve-hour shift that day that all my intuitive thoughts were confirmed. Jenna's call bell rang. I quickly tried to hand out some final medications, and complete my charting notes for the day before I went to see her. I had a feeling I would be with her for a while. When I entered her room and sat at her bedside, she grabbed my hand and held it. It was painful to see the fearful look in Jenna's eyes. It told the story I was writing inside my head all day long as I picked up on all the nuances and subtleties in her nonverbal language that I could read like a book. Jenna told me she felt scared. She was in a space she couldn't describe, and the disorientation frightened her.

She said to me, "I have been watching you."

I responded "I know you have been." I sat beside Jenna as she lay in bed, and I tried to comfort her, reassuring her I was right there and that I wouldn't leave her until she felt safe.

Jenna spoke to me further and said, "I look at you, and I see the passion in your eyes, and I wish I could trade places with you. I have never felt 'good enough' in this life."

My eyes filled with deep and penetrating emotion. I always thought Jenna was beautiful, both physically and in her heart as a person. I related to her fear and feeling of unworthiness, for I had felt the same way in my own life. It was interesting how I saw her and how she saw me. We both saw the beauty in each other but couldn't find it in ourselves.

Jenna was not the first woman to share this "not good enough" sentiment with me. I had heard it from many women who crossed my path during my health career. I can see it in women all over the world and in the media who don't even know it themselves yet. The signs are very easy to read for me now. If you remember, earlier in the book, Kevin Costner told us that even Whitney Houston, with all she had accomplished in life, felt "not good enough." Of course, my own mother felt this way before she died as well.

Every cell in my body filled with a rush of untamed emotion when I heard Jenna's words. All I could manage was to hold her, hug her, and tell her I would stay with her until she was not afraid any more. And I did.

Jenna died sometime in December, a month or so after these moments we shared. I knew that our time together had meaning for both of us. It would be a long time before I would forget Jenna and the resounding message and mirrored reflections that surfaced that day between us.

It wasn't until several months later that the full expression of the divine in the relationship I shared with Jenna was revealed to me. From the many encounters I have had with those on the other side, I have come to learn that the emotional upset or outpouring that overtakes us on occasion during these meetings happens because of the elevated vibration they carry and we collide with. I also believe that when those on the other side want to be heard or noticed, they ramp up the vibration to cause an emotional shift inside us so we can't miss their presence. It feels like walking into a wall of emotion that catches our full and undivided attention. Its entrance has to be grand or we would miss it in this busy and loud world.

One day in the spring, after Jenna's death, I drove my children to their first basketball practice. It was unusual for the practice to be held so far out of the vicinity of the YMCA. When we arrived, I brought the kids into the school gymnasium. I was drawn to the double doors that were to the left of the gym. A ray of beautiful golden yellow sun streamed through the glass doors as if welcoming me with open arms to bask in its healing light. Despite my usual tiredness, which seemed to carry an unnecessary weight, I was drawn toward it. The doors opened into a peaceful garden—just what I needed. I took a seat on a lovely bench to rest while the kids practiced.

As I looked up from my seat, I was stunned by the words covering the wall that surrounded the beautiful garden: "Jenna Glow ... lover of the earth."

Stopped in my tracks by spirit, I became awash with warm chills and uprising emotions at my core. Jenna had found a way to connect with me from heaven too! I wept almost inconsolably until the intense energy I felt inside spilled out of me and the knowing being downloaded penetrated my being. I knew Jenna was letting me know that she was with me in my moment of not feeling "good enough," and that she had come to realize that she was indeed "good enough."

Jenna was a teacher of children and a lover of the earth. A great legacy lives on in the beauty of the garden built to honor her, where her beautiful memory is imprinted on the scent of the flowers that grow there and the sun that shines down upon it. Even today as I write this story, I can feel her with me. She quietly reminds me to keep on loving myself and to keep living on purpose.

The Doors of Heaven

We tend to look at illness and disease with fear and panic instead of appreciating the brilliant attempts the body makes to communicate with us as it cleanses and rehabilitates through its own divine processes. I noted earlier that there are trillions of interactions going on inside of us that we never see, yet they save our lives over and over in every moment. When I became severely ill in October of

2010, initially I was unaware of the depth of illness and the profound healing that was taking place inside me.

At the time of my illness, I found out that my grandmother was dying and prepared myself for a six-hour trip to attend her funeral. My ninety-six year old grandmother was the last living connection I had to my mother. The physical pain I felt from the flu I thought I had and the emotional pain of the loss hit me like a ton of bricks, and I sobbed inconsolably for days before I traveled to get to the funeral. You can understand how the flu alone can make one feel awful; but even so, my instincts told me something else was happening to me. I chose to embrace the tears and allow them to flow.

My grandmother, Maude (Amanda) O'Malley, died on October 26, 2010. The night before her funeral, I tried to settle down to sleep but knew it wouldn't be too long before I awakened. This had been my pattern for the previous eight nights. Even the complete exhaustion I felt wouldn't allow me to rest. The total body pain I was feeling was only slightly numbed by the Advil I was taking. I wasn't really sure how much more pain—physical and emotional—I could take, as the lack of sleep on top of grieving was taking its toll. I kept my cell phone close by so I could use it as a light to get down the unfamiliar stairs at my sister's house while others slept during my wakefulness.

As predicted, shortly after I settled, I awoke. I was surprised to find a bright light shining in the corner of the room where the grand piano my niece Jenna played earlier the day before sat. There were no streetlights outside, so the source of the light was a mystery. I instantly thought of my grandmother, and then I knew she was contacting me, just to let me know she was with me. God knows I needed to be comforted, and I felt soothed by her presence.

I have had spirit manipulate light to get my attention before. When I got closer and inspected the light at the piano, I could see that my niece's computer, which sat on the piano ledge was in active mode, and the light shone from it. The computer had been in sleep mode when I went to bed, and it would be impossible for it to turn on by itself, so I was convinced it was my grandmother. After a cup of soothing tea and some toast, I grabbed some books about energy to flip through in my wakefulness. In response to a question asked in one of the books I read, I identified the heart as a symbol that has guided me in my life. I had a heart wall at my cottage, a heart room in my house, my original logo for my Successful Minds practice and now my REAL Beautiful logo both have hearts in them and I owned tons of heart jewelry (both necklaces and rings). I had no hesitation in answering that particular question.

The funeral the next morning was beautiful and sad, as would be expected. I walked by my grandmother's casket for the last time and said these words to her: "Grandma, I know you know where heaven is and what it is like. Please help me to understand it better. Please watch over me. I love you."

The next morning I got up after another night of interrupted sleep and gathered my belongings as best I could to prepare for the long journey home with my husband. As I sunk into the front seat of the car, I cuddled my fleece throw blanket up around my neck as if to demand some comfort. Very suddenly, I was overcome by an intense feeling of peace and freedom from the acute pain I had been experiencing for over a week now. I remember not wanting to move for fear the feeling would escape from me. I was absolutely grateful and desperate not to lose this healing moment in space and time. I could have cried I was so relieved. But I didn't. I just embraced the peace and comfort that infused my being.

Within moments, time seemed to disappear, as if I had been transported to another world. I was floating and looking at all of the clouds above me in the sky. I remember being astounded at how they all took on the shape of hearts. The sky was covered with hearts everywhere I looked. There were hearts upon hearts, countless layers of hearts, and even the occasional spaces of blue sky formed heart shapes. My thoughts were quickly guided to flashes of memories: the light by the piano the night before, the heart symbol I chose from the book, and asking my grandmother to show me heaven. After all these things computed, I had a knowing that my grandmother was speaking to me through all of the hearts in the sky. The warm healing flood that takes up residence inside me that I have come to recognize as spirit consumed me at that moment.

I began asking my grandmother questions, and she answered them in hearts. Bright white heart-shaped clouds I was directed to meant *yes*, and grey ones meant *no*. Soon, I felt transported beyond the clouds into a space in which I was with my grandmother. Or rather, I recall it more like the essence of my grandmother. I knew it was her, but I was feeling her from my heart and seeing her with unusual eyesight. My vision of her was not a physical one. Her body had no shape, but her presence was everywhere and all-consuming.

I remember feeling such indescribable peace that I didn't want to leave this space with her. If you knew me and the love I have for my children and my husband, you would realize that I would never want to be somewhere where they couldn't be with me. I believe heaven has many levels of vibration, and those who pass on live at higher vibrations that the living physical body cannot survive. These are the messages my grandmother had for me.

She told me, "This is what heaven feels like"—the answer to the question I asked her when I said good-bye to her at the funeral the day before. Next, she instructed me to "take better care of myself." When she said this, I knew she meant I had to love myself better and that not loving myself was making me sick. I was great at giving lots of love away as a nurse, mother of six children, sister, friend, and wife, but I knew I hadn't been doing a very good job of loving *me*. Ironically, I wasn't even sure how to go about doing that. I'd never thought about it.

Although I didn't really know how, I knew I had to figure it out if

I was going to survive this illness and move beyond it. This message of love echoes the one I received from Jenna Glow, and the ongoing messages of balance my mom guided me toward through the plant she gave me. It took a near-death experience for me to really heed the message. My hope is that it won't take this much for you to get it. I have experienced heaven without the heart stopping moments recorded on machines inside the hospital doors of an intensive care or emergency room documented to confirm such an account. My family and I were somehow spared this heart wrenching experience. This was a gift bestowed upon me. Just as one might die quietly in their sleep without pain and struggle, one might awake from death the same way carrying the strange and beautiful flowers they picked in heaven while they were there as proof. As I have come to know, the veil between heaven and earth is not what it seems, and we don't have to physically die to experience it. Heaven is not a place, but realm of higher vibrational energy.

> *There are many in the world dying for a piece of bread,*
> *but there are many more dying for a little love.*
> *—Mother Theresa*

Love Yourself

To close this chapter, and to honor the guidance I have received from heaven, I will tell you one of the most important things I have learned about love…

Sparkling Insight

Love has the power to heal and move mountains, just as the lack of it has the power to cause illness and block our way to the good stuff life has to offer. The secret, to find balance in the giving and receiving of love, is one of the greatest offerings of this book and in life. Self-love is a powerful hidden cure that is overlooked in our fast-paced world that leaves no time for it. The real magic comes when you actually set aside time for self-care/self-love activities. With time and practice, your vibrational energy begins to climb in response to these activities and then you link into the highest power that runs the universe. All that you need comes to you. Love vibrates high, as we have learned; and the balance of it vibrates the highest.

Because my mother gave me the Novena of the Rose prayer card just before she died, and had underlined some writing on the card in red, I was led to search for more information on St. Therese. In her autobiography, *The Story of a Soul*, I learned that St. Therese lived a short and simple hidden life of prayer before she died at the young age of twenty-four. She tells us that her purpose in life was not on earth, but in heaven to guide people to know Jesus. She also lets us in on a powerful secret in the book when she tells us, "What matters in life, is not great deeds, but great love." It is interesting that once again we are guided to love by a saint and spiritual master, and as we have already learned, love carries a high vibration.

St. Therese is known as "the greatest saint of modern times" and "a prodigy of miracles." She said she would send a shower of roses down from heaven to those who recite her prayer as a sign to them that the message has been heard (alluding to our ability to connect with those who pass on). Countless roses come to my door— literally and figuratively—and represent the answer from heaven to the prayer I am saying. Saying prayers with great intention and dedication like this novena requires, *(it is to be recited for nine days at the same time every day highlighting the power the act of dedication and commitment can have to activate miracles)* with a genuine heart, reflects the knowledge we are learning about how to raise vibrational energy within our cells and understanding it in a new way through the sacred science behind the power of prayer. It is an ongoing novena for me. I have chosen it as a daily *sacred sadhana* or dedicated daily practice that supports one's life; you will learn more about this in chapter 15. The novena continues to bless my life with the unseen forces that miracles contain.

This prayer is obviously extraordinarily special to me because my mom gave it to me on a prayer card before she died. It has also been a divine guidepost on multiple occasions. I am honored to share this sacred prayer with you for your own use. If you are interested in learning more about St. Therese, visit the website at littleflower.org.

The prayer card my mother gave me had two prayers on it, and I have always recited them both. As related above, say this novena for nine consecutive days, at the same time of day.

Miraculous Invocation to St. Therese

O glorious Saint Therese, whom almighty God has raised up to aid and counsel mankind, I implore your Miraculous Intercession. So powerful are you in obtaining every need of body and soul, our Holy Mother Church proclaims you a "Prodigy of Miracles … the Greatest Saint of Modern Times." Now I reverently beseech you to answer my petition (mention intention here) and to carry out your heaven doing good upon earth … of letting fall from heaven a shower of roses. Henceforth dear Little Flower, I will fulfill your plea "to be made known everywhere," and I will never cease to lead others to Jesus through you. Amen.

My Novena Rose Prayer

O Little Therese of the Child Jesus, please pick for me a rose from the heavenly gardens and send it to me as a message of love.

O Little Flower of Jesus, ask God to grant me the favors I now place with confidence in your hands (state your intentions here).

St. Therese, help me to always believe as you did in God's great love for me, so that I might imitate your "Little Way" each day. Amen

Sparkling Insight

When your intention has been heard in heaven you will receive roses/flowers or be drawn mystically to a rose (photo, rose bush in a garden and so on) as a sign that your intention has been answered. These events are also a message to you that you have made contact with heaven; a beautiful thing.

More Self-Love Ideas

For more ideas on how to love yourself better and know that you are always "good enough," follow these sparkling insights from women who are a part of the REAL Beautiful Movement with me.

From Colleen Sidun, intuitive healer and founder of Living on the Inside on Facebook: "Think of how good you feel when your house is clean, uncluttered, and fresh! It's funny that we do this so naturally in our homes but never take the time to do this within ourselves. Every experience that we harbor holds energy. This energy resides in our cells, minds, and organs, and as we grow, our bodies become increasingly full of baggage. We become sluggish and stuffed and our 'original' energy is smothered. In many cases, the result is anxiety, depression, and/or illness. It is for these reasons that I began to use tools like visualization or meditation. By using your mind and imagination, you can let go of old thoughts and beliefs in order to reestablish a clear state of being. Use a vacuum to suck it out, a lint brush to collect it, or a magnet to evict it. It doesn't matter how you choose to do it; the exercise of using your mind to clear out your body repetitively will give you a fresh direction in life. So open your mind. It is time to air out the house!"

From Jessica Van Til, public health and safety student at Ryerson University, Toronto, Ontario: "It doesn't matter that many people live within concrete jungles and spend most of their days working in an office; humans are still deeply connected to nature. People may forget because today's society disconnects them from it; but they are reminded when they notice how beautiful a flower is, or how calming the trees in the park are. This also relates to studies that show patients who have flowers in their rooms heal faster. This relationship we have with nature has been ingrained in our species over centuries of living off the land to survive. In 1984, Edward O. Wilson wrote an entire book on this relationship called *Biophilia*, which means 'love for all living things.' So my advice is to reconnect with that love that is so much a part of every one of us by taking a walk in a park or by filling your house with as many plants as you can. No matter how you do it, take time to connect with the positive, calming energy that nature radiates."

From Aime Hutton @ awakeninggoddess.com: "Dance. Every morning, put on your favorite piece of music and dance!"

From Colleen Dinan: "Spend an hour outdoors every day, rain or shine, and breathe. As a dog owner, I have no choice, and it has been the best form of meditation, exercise, and empowerment."

From Becca Heath, English student at the University of Western Ontario: "Whenever I go for a walk, I imagine that every breath I take in is cleansing every negative thought I have had out of me. I inhale good healing energy and exhale all the negative energy that weighs me down. I feel better … and lighter!"

To add to these sparkling insights, I thought I would share some further ideas about how you could love yourself, for those of you who are not familiar or comfortable with this concept.

- Every practice and insight in this book breeds self-love on a cellular level. Every action we take to uplift our vibrational energy in the mind, body, and spirit is a loving practice.

- Counterbalance negative self-talk by telling yourself "I love you" while you look at yourself in a mirror. It feels weird at first, but you will feel the power when you say it.

- Recite the "I am bountiful, blissful, beautiful" mantra potent with the sacred words given to us directly by Yogi Bhajan shared in this book and on my website. It will penetrate you on a cellular level and help you to celebrate who you are because he created it masterfully and scientifically to have this effect inside you.

- Hug yourself. The action of crossing your arms over your chest guides your hands to the spleen acupressure points on the sides of the body towards the lower ribs under the armpit and directly under each breast *(spleen points discussed in chapter 8).* Massage these points to improve your health and well-being and uplift your vibrational energy while you feel the healing comfort of your own hug.

- Take time to sip on a cup of healing tea or any healing drink and breathe in life force deeply just for you. Every deep breath offers life and the gifts shared by higher vibrations. Every breath adds up over time.

- Make yourself a healthy meal and send love into the ingredients and then reflect as you take the love into your body.

- Forgive yourself and feel the warmth that tingles inside you when you do this.

- Dedicate fifteen minutes of every day to breathing consciously and deeply.

- Massage a part of your body that you dislike and tell it you love it. Your cells are listening.

- Stay away from watching or looking at media that devalues women. Misrepresentation calls us to boycott the media and products that don't have our best interests at heart.

- Make another woman feel beautiful for who she is.

- Sit in the sun and take in its healing light. It is a gift.

- Join the REAL Beautiful Movement and receive a downloadable heart that you can add your own sparkles to. Keep one heart for you and give sparkled hearts away to other women so they can link into the knowledge that makes them shine and connect to their own beauty, power, healing, magic, and miracles! Remember, sharing the knowledge of this power is the secret that causes your own vibrational energy to skyrocket!

Chapter 12

Enlightened Master of Our Time: Gregg Braden

A miracle that is possible for anyone is possible for everyone.
—Gregg Braden

More Sacred Insights

*W*ITH A CAREER HISTORY THAT is far-reaching across the depths of understanding required to be an expert in the language of computers, Gregg Braden journeys even farther and wider as he embraces the knowledge in the language of the universe. The *New York Times* best-selling author of several life-changing books—you can view all of his work at his website at greggbraden.com—Gregg closes the gap between science and spirituality as he bridges ancient and new wisdom that brings the power to create miracles, blessings, beauty, and a bright future if we are willing to learn.

Some of the secrets that uncover the truth behind who we really are lie hidden in the forgotten texts, high mountain villages, and remote monasteries Gregg has sought out, studied, and researched. He teaches us the ways to manifest the heaven on earth many of us long for, though it continues to slip through our hands, and he brings attention to the energy contained within our thoughts, emotions, feelings, and the divine field of energy that is a part of us.

Thoughts, Feelings, and Emotions

There is a space that exists with us and around us where angels sing and love pours forth from the heart of the universe.
—Snatam Kaur

Snatam Kaur reminds us in this quote above of a feild of energy or "space" inside and around us that we can connect to and move in and out of at our own will. In this space, the energy of the highest power, God, the divine source or the "heart of the universe" as she calls it, lives. When we connect with it, heaven is revealed to us, and the experience of heaven is felt. Gregg shows us some powerful ways to connect with this space or energy field, in line with the other practices and technologies I share inside this book.

In his documentary film *The Science of Miracles*, Gregg explains the science behind the energy of our thoughts, feelings, and emotions and how we can direct the vibrations they hold to light the spark that brings magic to life inside and outside of us. Whether you want to heal, renew a relationship, receive abundance, solve the mysteries of life, or know the way to success, the miracles wait to be awakened. I have created a formula to relate Gregg's findings to help simplify his brilliant insights and nudge the experience of miracles into your life a little faster.

Gregg uncovers the hidden secret behind prayer similar to the sacred scripture related under the quote from Gregg; both of which are found ahead. The feelings we create in our heart speak the language that the universe understands. If the vibration of that feeling is high enough, it connects with the vibration of the highest power that manifests magic and miracles, and answered prayers. Once again, we can understand why this information might be hidden away and kept secret by those who are unconscious and self-serving, as discussed in chapter 10. This knowledge may remain difficult to believe and "too good to be true" for some, but it has the capacity to transform a life instantly in the moment the connection is made. For those who haven't experienced it yet, it may require consistent dedication to the secrets Gregg shows us, along with other practices shared throughout this book, if these practices are not already a part of your ways of living and being. I think it depends on where your energy resonates in this moment. You have to account for your own ways of thinking, feeling, and emoting, and then be willing to open up to the higher wisdom of enlightened masters like Gregg and the beautiful and sacred texts that surround us to unlock the secrets.

We must feel the feeling as if the prayer is already answered.
—Gregg Braden

So I tell you, whatever you ask for in prayer,
believe that you have received it and it will be yours.
—Mark 11:24

Sparkling Insight

As the insightful quotes above tell us, we must speak to
the universe with our thoughts, feelings, and emotions
in a way that reflects that we have already received that
which we intend. This practice requires us to become
in tune and in control of our thoughts, feelings, and
emotions because they draw matching energies to us.

The technologies that follow are examples of the ways we can direct our thoughts, emotions, and feelings to manifest miracles, blessings that uplift our vibrational energy, REAL beauty, and the hope for a brighter future in our lives—all thanks to Gregg's passion for understanding the power of our energy being better.

Making Miracles Happen

I created a formula for miracles from Gregg's findings. Find a place where you can get quiet and reflective so that you can practice bringing the vibration of your thoughts, emotions, and feelings together and in line with an intention of your choice. If you know your body is pretty filled up with negativity, allow time to practice this formula and align your physical vibration with high energy sources like; love, beauty, gratitude, honesty, kindness, peace, and that of the miracles you hope for —and feel the feeling that each of these states of being contain. Practice letting go of lower vibrational energy (greed, hatred, anxiety, fear, jealousy, guilt, unworthiness, and so on) to encourage the changes in energy required to make the formula work. Over time, as these ways of thinking, feeling, and emoting become a steady part of your being, you will be able to apply the formula with less effort. With daily focus and practice in this exercise, I have experienced some moments that have brought almost instant miracles. It has become my proof that Gregg's findings are accurate.

Remember, if our feelings have the power to speak to the universe and the universe responds with an equal manifestation in a physical or tangible way or experience, then our power to create our own beauty and all things is unlimited.

The Miracle Formula

High-energy thoughts + high-energy heartfelt emotions: creates high-energy feelings = MIRACLES

What are the things that would feel like a miracle to you in your life? Start aligning your thoughts and heartfelt emotions to these things so the feelings that result speak to the universe and draw them to you. Do you want to create the miracle of healing, bliss, peace, success, higher consciousness, supportive relationships, financial support, love, a sense of purpose? It is your choice. Start by choosing the miracle you wish to align with. Your thoughts and emotions must be heartfelt—meaningful and given your full attention—if you want to create feelings that draw to you the things you want.

> *Cross your hands over your heart while you gain focus on the thoughts and emotions you want to create that will align with your miracle of choice.*

Here's an example of how the miracle formula works:

The miracle request is to feel beautiful and empowered!

Thoughts

Say these words to yourself: I am bountiful, blissful, and beautiful. I am so grateful to be filled with abundance/bounty, bliss/happiness, and feel beautiful on all levels!

+

Emotions

Create the emotions that match your thoughts above by seeing yourself with a sense of pride. Honor every part of your being from your heart. Hug yourself, forgive yourself, and tell yourself you deserve happiness, empowerment, abundance and all things beautiful. Feel the experience of all of these things in your life right now, as if you already have them. What would that feel like? These efforts create the feelings that match the things you ask the universe for with your new language and help you saturate your being with the energy they hold. Feel what you think bountifulness, blissfulness and beauty feel like so you can become them. Always add a sense of gratitude for being given these things to intensify your results.

+

Feelings

All of the thoughts and emotions you create above become the feelings that create a vibration inside of you and communicate the same vibration to the universe.

=

Magic and Miracles

When you begin to feel and believe you are bountiful, blissful, and beautiful consistently from your heart, every cell inside your body and wave of energy in the universe listens! Matching vibrations attract one another and miracles happen!

If you watch Gregg Braden's documentary *The Science of Miracles*, you can witness this miracle formula in action as an actual cancerous tumor disappears when highly trained "feeling practitioners" create the thoughts and emotions that dissolve it. If we train ourselves to become experts like these individuals, we can create similar miracles.

Gregg reminds us that the intelligent field that surrounds us mirrors back to us the collective balance of the energy that is contained in the feelings we hold from moment to moment, and not only affect us directly, but the world at large with the ripple effect the vibrations we carry inside of us send out to the world. This powerful internal technology we own becomes the science behind the miracles we experience and create in our lives. That we own this power is a miracle in itself!

The Gift of the Blessing

Another powerful technology Gregg shares with us from his research is The Gift of the Blessing. Science reveals the power we have to protect ourselves from the hurt that happens in daily life by embracing the truth of our energy being and learning how to redirect the path of hurt—and the energy that *feeling hurt* can potentially hold inside every cell in the body if we are not careful. In the process of embracing hurt by blessing it, we uplift our vibrations and breed compassion.

Science relates that if we don't find a way to resolve and let go of the things that hurt us, we are at risk for lower levels of health and well-being, and our power to vibrate at higher levels is negatively affected. Before you begin the blessing technology below, you must let go of the need to feel or believe that if someone hurts you, your only choice is to make them pay, or pay them back in return with more hurt. The "an eye for an eye" mentality has to be forgotten.

On the contrary, we must become more forgiving, accepting, and compassionate of the so-called wrongdoer or hurtful event.

This doesn't mean you have to sit down and have dinner with them to forgive them. Remember, we are trying to protect ourselves from harmful energy. But, if we embrace hurt by recognizing it for what it is—a chemical disturbance in the energy field that lives in and around us—we hold the power to stop the ripple effect from the outside with the chemistry on the inside and thus neutralize the effect of the energy of the hurt altogether.

The Blessing Process

1. When something happens that makes you feel hurt, bless the situation, circumstance, person, or event. To bless someone or something does not mean you condone, agree, or consent—it only accepts and honors the divine nature in all things and people. For example, if you see someone littering, are on the receiving end of hurtful words, or see someone mistreating someone else, take a moment to say, "I bless this person or situation for the hurt it causes me, him or her, and the environment."

2. During the blessing, it is critical that you come to know and accept that everything and everyone that exists is a part of the divine power within and outside of us all. We are all divine in nature, without exception, as we are all connected to the nature of our energy being and the energy of the universe itself. You must believe in the truth that there is only one source from which all things and beings are created, even those individuals and events that hurt us. You have to trust that all things happen in a divine order you may not understand. All you have to do is acknowledge this wisdom and accept it as truth as you bless the individual or situation causing you to feel hurt.

Sparkling Insight

The act of blessing in this way helps protect us from the chemical changes that could result from the hurt and affect our health and well-being. This result is similar in nature to the healing power of an act of kindness. Research demonstrates that an act of kindness can increase the immunity of the giver, receiver, and observer of the act of kindness. And if we continue to remember that our feelings influence the chemistry in our bodies, we can understand the power of the blessing more clearly.

3. Next, be sure to bless yourself for having to experience the hurt. Our cells listen to us when we are gentle and caring. For example, you could say to yourself, "I bless myself for having to hear those hurtful words. I deserve love and will not allow this negative energy to affect my being."

4. As you complete the final step in the blessing process, be in tune with the sense of peace, bliss, warmth, and tingling you will experience as your cells fill with the higher vibrations. This is your reward and a sign of your power to heal and uplift yourself. This exercise is a reminder that blessing things instead of being hurt by them, feeds the mind, body, and spirit with healing energy and higher vibrations. This result reminds me of how we are told to love our enemies. Could it be that one of the greatest spiritual masters of time, Jesus, guided us to forgive and bless those who hurt us so we could keep higher vibrations in our bodies too?

5. You can extend this blessing beyond things that are happening in the moment to those things that have hurt you in the past. Remember to observe and experience the release, warmth, or tingling that takes place in your body in the moment of the

blessing. It may require some time to identify the positive feeling you experience, but it chemically and scientifically happens, and this is all you need to know. In time and with experience with the blessing technology, you will feel the changes that take place in mind, body, and spirit more easily.

The Power of Beauty

Beauty awakens only when we invite it into our lives.
—Gregg Braden

The concept of beauty so often defined in only superficial and skin-deep descriptions of the thin, flawless perfection demanded of women in our Western society completely misses the true definition and essence of the REAL beauty we have access to with our energy-being powers. The power of this kind of beauty will make our skin glow, lessen our wrinkles, and fill our lives with beautiful people, places, and things. Think of the money you will save when you cultivate your own beauty from the inside out. Just as feeling good vibrations and the ingestion of healthy food awakens beauty, so does the Beauty Prayer I share with you below.

In *Secrets of the Lost Mode of Prayer: The Hidden Power of Beauty, Blessing, Wisdom, and Hurt,* Gregg Braden writes, "Recent discoveries in Western science now add to a growing body of evidence suggesting that beauty is a transformative power. More than simply an adjective that describes the colors of a sunset or a rainbow following a late-summer storm, beauty is an experience—specifically, beauty is *our* experience. Humans are believed to be the only species of life on earth with the capability of perceiving beauty in the world around them, and within the experiences of their lives. Through our experience of beauty we're given the power to change the feelings that we have in our bodies. Our feelings, in turn, are directly linked to the world beyond our bodies."

The Beauty Prayer

If we live, breathe, eat, sleep, think, and feel beauty we become the vibration of beauty, and thus draw all that is beautiful to us magnetically. In *Secrets of the Lost Mode of Prayer*, Gregg shares a Beauty Prayer utilized by the Navajo Indians, which demonstrates their wisdom of the inner chemistry we all own to draw beauty to us when we saturate mind, body, and spirit with it. The prayer reminds us that, to live and be beautiful, we must become beauty. The prayer directly speaks to this truth by stating the elements required to manifest all things beautiful in life.

The prayer translates from Navajo words Nizhonigoo bil iina into:

> The beauty that you live with,
>
> The beauty that you live buy,
>
> The beauty upon which you base your life.

Let's manifest beauty in our lives together. Our ways of living and being create all types of beauty if we choose.

The Isaiah Effect

In the fourth and final secret I share from Gregg Braden's wisdom, we learn that there are multiple futures that wait for you and me to choose from. In his book *The Isaiah Effect,* Gregg strengthens our magic powers by guiding us to the ways of thinking, emoting, feeling, living, and being that can design the future we wish for over one we don't. To have the power of our own vibration linking with that of the universe creates a potent elixir to orchestrate the elements we choose for our future in every moment that elapses. With pen in hand, you rewrite your future in the fruitful moments of "the now." You will feel as though you have a magic wand in your hand that redirects certain circumstances and synchronicities to align with a new future of your choice.

I can't tell you how powerful this knowledge is. Why are we not being taught this in school?

Sparkling Insight

There is no power greater than the one that intentionally and consciously joins forces and unites with the highest divine vibration of the universe. Enlightened sage and spiritual master Patanjali reminds us that "dormant forces, faculties, and talents come alive" when we take action and collaborate our lives with the highest power. It is the unseen power we tap into that releases the magic into the air. Unexpected miracles seem to happen effortlessly, and we find greatness within us we never thought possible. This ever-present infusion of magic effortlessly redraws events, circumstances, opportunities, and synchronicities that make our new and improved futures unfold before our eyes.

Live and Breathe Your Future

Make a list and decide what your future will hold, and then get started becoming your future as you have learned in some of the secret practices shown to you in this chapter. Are you doing something in this moment that will create the future you want? Make a list and start living and breathing your future, and it will come to you. Don't forget about the unseen forces that will help you after you get started (a powerful secret many people don't know).

Saturate your mind, body, and spirit with that which you want to exist. Live and breathe it and expect it to show up! The beauty behind this truth is that when we begin doing what it takes to make the future we want happen, the unseen forces Patanjali speaks of are activated to support us on our quest. The energy in the committed feelings we have is a key that unlocks the secret powers inside of us and the universe. These vibrational frequencies speak the language the universe understands as it designs the future we intend with our own mind, body, and spirit!

A magical thing happened while I was researching *The Isaiah Effect* for this book. I applied it to my own life as I synchronously came up against a situation I needed to change. I had only six months earlier recovered from my almost fatal pneumonia when my chest began to feel congested, just days before a very important speaking engagement. I thought of *The Isaiah Effect* and put it to the test. Being a health educator, I know many ways to support health and healing. I thought about all of the insights and technologies I share in this book and a few outside of it, and created a schedule for three days that would rewrite a future that appeared to be going in the direction of being ill for my important event. I added the heartfelt energy of intention in behind my schedule of healing strategies *(I created the vision and feelings that matched the recovery I wanted inside me, I applied the 'three thumps' practice I had learned from energy medicine, I listened to healing mantras, steamed my respiratory system by inhaling a magic healing potion I created that simmered gently on my stove, I prepared myself for the workshop I was to deliver and intensely believed it was possible to heal)!*

Plain and simple, it worked. I did feel the unseen forces come to my aid once I got started as they gave the extra infusion of magic that seemed to effortlessly undo any traces of illness. I even had to adjust my level of belief a couple times, as it wavered. In the end, every hint of illness left me, and in fact, I skipped the recovery days and slipped right into full vibrant health for the presentation.

How will you change your future today? What thoughts, beliefs, feelings, emotions, and practices do you keep in your hearts that are creating your future in this moment?

Sparkling Insight

Let's revisit the message in the sacred quote that follows and remember the power we own to create the future and all of the things we want in life with the energy in and around us.

So I tell you, whatever you ask for in prayer, believe that you have received it and it will be yours.

—*Mark 11:24*

I want to thank Gregg Braden for living on purpose and discovering these beautiful hidden secrets that hold the power to magically transform our lives. I am grateful to have met up with your energy and insight, similar to all of the wisdom of the other enlightened masters and experts I share in this book.

I consider Gregg's work to be a treasure and would encourage you to own and study his works. I continue to be astounded at the overflowing amount of beautiful secrets he shares so willingly in every book, CD, and DVD. They are a wealth of knowledge for us all. I commend Gregg's effort to help rewrite the science books of our future so that our present and next generations can live REAL Beautiful lives because of him.

Chapter 13

The Secret Energy of the Heart

When we form heart-centered beliefs within our bodies, in the language of physics we're creating the electrical and magnetic expression of them as waves of energy, which aren't confined to our hearts or limited by the physical barrier of our skin and bones. So clearly we're "speaking" to the world around us in each moment of every day through a language that has no words: the belief-waves of our hearts.
—Gregg Braden

You are becoming the song of your heart...
how beautiful it is, as the flower blossoms forth.
—Snatam Kaur and Peter Kater

Heart Power

*W*E ARE ALL FAMILIAR WITH the important role the heart plays physiologically and biologically, as it is like an engine that supplies the rest of the body with its vital life-giving essence, blood. It circulates and moves this essence through all of our cells so that they may be nurtured, healed, rejuvenated, and recreated from moment to moment. Miraculously, the heart has an intelligence of its own and can identify and react to the energy it connects with through emotions and stress, both positive and negative, and ultimately influence the activity or energy patterns of the heart.

The study of heart-rate variability through the Institute of HeartMath proves over and over that our heart responds to the emotions and experiences of our lives through its heart-rate variability (HRV)—that is, the rhythm of our heartbeat. Heart coherence exists when balance is achieved psychophysiologically. Practices related in this book—such as meditation, prayer, sacred and scientific words, and carefully orchestrated emotions—magically soothe and balance our heart's rhythm to improve our well-being and induce coherence.

Thoughts, feelings, emotions, and behaviors affect the beat of your heart. Positive influences like appreciation bring healthy balance to the beat, while mental and emotional stresses disrupt balance and health. According to the Institute of HeartMath's website at heartmath.org, "The research shows that the greater an individual's level of coherence, the more efficient and harmonious the body's cardiovascular, nervous, hormonal and immune systems function."

Just as we have the power to influence the pattern of our heartbeat, we can affect the level of coherence of another person's heart when we are within conversational distance. The power the heart has to heal has been known to many of us through our own experience of being in loving relationships with others.

I recall an incident when my children were younger. As they played with their cousins, an argument broke out between two of the children. My nephew, who was only four years old at the time and remains very intuitive even today, shouted out in response to the arguing, "My heart is beating slower." As we learn from heart science, a heart that beats too slowly would be considered out of healthy coherence. This is an example of how our bodies try to signal to us, if we are in tune within, that something is not right. If we listen more closely to the messages our bodies send us, it will guide us to an understanding of what we need to change to encourage this balance. In this instance, my nephew Danny's coherence was being negatively influenced by the hurt/upset taking place, but it could return to a healthier balance if the individuals who were arguing forgave one another and hugged.

You can likely remember a positive influence that brought your heart into perfect balance in the sense of the harmony we feel when we truly experience love from another or for another in life. I remember feeling strong, happy, healthy, and at peace when I fell in love with my husband. I feel the same when I think about how much I love my children.

The Heart, Our Love, and Our Health

The heart has been referred to as the fourth chakra or energy center of the body. The electromagnetic force of energy it emits is much more potent than even the brain. Some researchers feel it should be considered the first brain instead of the third, after the brain and the stomach. The heart chakra (Anahata chakra) involves the heart, lungs, and thymus. The colors associated with the heart chakra are green, pink, and gold. The heart brings circulation, the lungs breath, and the thymus, immunity to the body. Most interestingly, when we become unbalanced in the love we give and receive, these organs are affected.

My own immunity was so depleted when I developed severe pneumonia and had my near-death experience. The message from my grandmother in heaven was that I needed to love and care for myself better; something I knew in my own heart had been missing for most of my life. In the end, it makes sense that my body responded with pneumonia to my relentless lack of self-love and care. My depleted heart rate, breath, and immunity were reflections of this truth and my body's way of communicating what needed to be addressed in my life. As you are coming to realize from reading this book, listening to the messages our mind, body, and spirit have for us is one of the greatest powers we own! Any health issues connected to the lungs, thymus or immunity are emotionally connected to the balance of love we maintain in our lives. It is important to observe the balance between the love we give to others and the love we give and receive for ourselves. If you are out of balance with these two ways of being, the heart rhythms become out of sync with the rest of the mind, body, and spirit, and then your well-being on many levels is negatively affected.

Women are some of the best examples I know of individuals who are so good at giving love. It is bred into our human design, as we are the mothers of the world. Because of this, we greatly identify with nurturing others as part of our biological and societal role. From my own personal experience and witnessing the same in other women, I believe it is difficult for most women to get the balance between giving and receiving love right. I believe the pattern of giving love more than receiving it is why many women feel so tired when they give instead of feeling rejuvenated.

Just look at the strong messages in the mass media that portray women over and over as scantily clad sex objects for another's enjoyment. This repetitive message filled with the lower vibrations of dishonor, keeps women weak, disempowered, and at lower levels of health and well-being. We are taught in all religions, social learning, and even in energy topics discussed around the globe that love is the key to happiness and abundance. Why then are so many 'love' givers feeling abused, tired, angry, and depleted?

Sparkling Insight

We are reminded again that finding the balance between giving and receiving love is the greatest secret the power of the heart holds.

This knowledge allows you the freedom to step away from giving to others for a while and bring some balance to this matter by giving a little love to yourself and learning to receive you own love as well as love from others. As related in the ways to self-love listed in chapter 11, in the meditation that follows, and throughout this book; loving ourselves is the greatest love and secret of all.

I think it is our tendency to underestimate the power of the heart in our lives or any other organ in our bodies, but our body speaks to us if we choose to listen. My near-death experience with pneumonia was my body's way of catching my full attention and saying it was time for me to start loving myself, instead of everyone else. I find it synchronistic that the message sent to me by my grandmother when I met up with her in heaven was that I needed to take better care of myself and start loving myself. I knew this already. I just wasn't fully listening before the clarity that came through during my near-death experience when I had pneumonia. Unknowingly at the time, I had been listening to vibration raising music that was already at work inside me making the necessary changes and bringing the insight to me that would change my life forever. I was healing from the inside out and on a self-love journey that required some balance. Go ahead.

You have my permission to listen to the self-love messages you have been receiving and love yourself in a balanced way right now in this moment; you and I both know you deserve it.

I have combined much of the sacred science shared in this book into one beautiful and loving meditation below. This meditation has the power to create self-love miracles. It will bring healing, health, and balance to the ways you give and receive love in your daily living and being.

The Eleven-Second Self-Love Miracle Heart Meditation

The healing technologies included in this meditation are:

- breath/*pranayama* therapy
- heart-coherence technology
- visualization
- numerology
- chakra technology/science
- the science behind meditation
- mudra science (hand postures): *Our hands are magic. Hand postures or mudras send energy messages to the mind, body, and spirit and open the flow of energy in the body and in the universe.*
- the science of the mantra *(sacred words that carry a vibration)*

  To begin, remember to settle into your sacred space that heightens the effects of any meditation—you will learn this in chapter 15.

1. Sit in a comfortable position with a straight spine and neck, close your eyes, and apply *Padma Mudra*.

Padma Mudra (Lotus Flower): Bring your hands in front of your heart chakra and place the heels of the palms of each hand together while you create space between the palms above this point *(similar to prayer pose, but your palms will only touch at the heel of the palms).* Spread your fingers out and slightly curve them as they stretch upward while you keep a hollow space inside the palm area. While the heels of your palms continue to touch, let your pinkie fingers and the sides of your thumbs on both hands touch, or slightly touch.

Padma Mudra Health Benefits:

- *awakens self-healing power*
- *weakens the ego (your false self)*
- *calms the mind*
- *improves the health of the heart and pericardium (the membrane that surrounds the heart)*
- *brings balance to the immune system and strengthens the lungs*
- *opens the heart chakra*
- *encourages a connection to the divine/highest power*

2. Breathe in through your nose with a steady and deep breath that fills your lungs completely from top to bottom for eleven seconds. Gently retain this breath inside for 11 seconds.

3. Release the breath slowly and steadily through your nose to completely empty your lungs as you count to eleven. As you release the breath, take note of the warm tingle you feel in your body. This experience is living proof of the chemical exchange taking place in your body because of the essence and power of life force that transforms and rebuilds us.

4. Hold this breath out to the count of eleven and then begin your next sequence of breaths.

5. Once you get comfortable with this meditation add the following: as you inhale begin to see the color green, pink, or gold flowing into and filling your heart as you expand your lungs. Hold this color in your heart for the eleven seconds as you retain your breath and then allow the color to flow out of you as you let your breath go. Along with visualizing the color green, pink, or gold filling your heart as you breathe in, remember to continue to expand your lungs fully from top to bottom.

6. Finally, add the following sacred mantra to guide you to the secret truth of your being. Repeat *Sat Nam* (pronounced 'Sut Numb') out loud or in silence throughout the meditation. You can also use the powerful mantra from Yogi Bhajan "I am bountiful, blissful and beautiful I am" or "I am empowered when I balance self-love with selfless love." Try a different mantra each time you do this meditation or use one 40 times before you move to the next one.

Health Benefits:

- *provides all of the benefits of Padma Mudra listed*
- *improves holistic health in the mind, body, and spirit*
- *connects us to our divine power*
- *increases our self-love and the celebration of self*
- *balances our giving and receiving of love*
- *brings forth the truth to our being*

Chapter 14

The Secret Energy in Flowers

If we could see the miracle of a single flower clearly,
our whole life would change.
—Buddha

Flowers offer us so much more than color, scent, and beauty ...
all plants and trees possess vibrational energies that resonate with our
own to heal mind and body.
—Barbara Olive

Flower Essence: What is It?

I SEE FLOWERS AS ONE OF many wonders of the world. In the contemplation of a rose—my absolute favorite flower—I have been awed not only by its beauty and fragrance but by the mystery each one holds and the divine magic that roses have brought into my life. How does it come to express itself so regally from the confines of a woody stem and root bulb? To understand the mystery behind all of the transformations that take place to make a flower bloom and reveal its delicate beauty so tightly bound in a bud that magically unfolds over time expressing its full capacity, is one of life's beautiful miracles.

Yet even beyond this awesome wonder, we can go deep within the flower to capture its vibrational energy or essence, and then even more beautiful secrets are revealed to us. Once the essence or energy of a flower is transferred from a flower into a healing elixir, we can consume this energy so that its vibration can blend with our own: the vibration gently and gracefully penetrates the mind, body, and spirit to find ways to bring balance to it. It is as if the flower energy speaks to us in a language of its own. Whether there is an emotional release that unwraps blocked energy or an opportunity presents itself synchronously to support balancing the unsettled emotions and energy within, we beautifully find the balance we were seeking. Like a magic elixir created with the petals of the flower and the glowing power of the sun, the essence of flowers create miracles that bring about REAL Beautiful ways of living and being. And as with all things in life, including our own brilliant being, when the real truth of our being and that of all things is explored, we consistently find that vibrational energy is at the heart of all things.

Dr. Edward Bach, a bacteriologist, physician, and pathologist, is well known for his work in the 1920s and 1930s to discover the powerful and healing capabilities of flowers to gently and beautifully support our emotional health and well-being. He was intuitively guided to thirty-eight flowers and their combinations to help ease and transform emotional imbalances that negatively affect our lives. Arthur Bailey, an electrical engineer and healer, intuitively discovered flower remedies beyond the thirty-eight discovered by Bach and improved the range of remedies that are available to lovingly heal the emotional challenges we face throughout life on even deeper realms connected to our consciousness. By capturing the energy contained within a flower, the vibration of that energy is transferred into our being when we take flower essence. I am so grateful to have been guided to this divine, captivating, magnetic, and most beautifully exquisite therapy.

Flower essence expert Barbara Olive goes back further into the history and mystery inside flowers in her book *The Flower Healer*, writing that "The healing power of flowers has been lovingly used for centuries, across the world and throughout civilizations. The ancient Greeks and Egyptians held Nature itself as a religious symbol, and flowers, plants, and trees were deemed to be a gift from the gods and to hold many powers of virtue, luck, love, and divine protection from evil. Temples and sacred places were often built in areas of outstanding beauty, and flowers where believed to have spiritual and supernatural powers."

Once again, ancient knowledge becomes new to us in our day and time, as in the cycles of life and history. When we are sure to utilize knowledge and wisdom from those who have lived before us, we uncover some truths below the surface of flowers and all things that allow us to experience higher and more beautiful realms of living and being previously unknown to us.

The Beauty in the Making of Flower Essence

Every flower carries its own unique energy. The creator of flower essence is intuitively guided to a flower and its specific healing power. The vibrational energy of a flower is captured through placing the flower petals, roots, stems, and heads into crystal bowls of spring water to bathe in the energy of the sun or the moon. The spirit and energy of the flower becomes infused in the now healing spring water to create what is called *flower essence*. Each and every flower's healing power is determined intuitively by the creator of the essence, as the creators are individuals who have developed the ability to connect to other realms.

As we each have our own special purpose in this world, I am so grateful to Dr. Bach, who first discovered this beautiful therapy, and for Barbara Olive, who has the insight and fortitude to follow the inner voice that guided her to produce her own beautiful flower essences. This therapy is gentle, effective, healing, and comforting to me. You can purchase any of Barbara's beautiful flower essences at essenceworld.com. You can also search "flower essences" on the Internet and find a plethora of essence creators. I refer you to Dr. Bach's flower-essence remedies and Bailey's name-brand essences in this book because I feel they are readily available in Canada in most health-food stores. With advancing technology, it is obviously easy to order online if this is your preference.

A healing therapy can't get more beautiful for a woman—seeking the help of our beloved flowers to bring us healing and vibrancy. So perfect, isn't it? Once again, as with anything we do, we have to be consistent and mindful in the use of any of the healing therapies we choose, or their vibrational energy will not be able to have its most powerful effect.

Sparkling Insight

Even the essence of a flower knows when we are making its presence sacred. If we reflect, honor, intend, and focus

on the flower essence of our choice its power intensifies.
You will learn more about making things sacred in the
next chapter.

I chose my top REAL Beautiful flower essences to share with you in this book. There are many others available, and combinations of essences that can be taken as well. Every store that sells flower essences provides a chart to explain the healing support each essence offers. You become the chooser of the one that will work for you, for you are the one who knows deep inside your priorities and needs. Don't be afraid to be honest when you choose. If you know you are choosing remedies around the one you really know you need, then it is likely the essence you choose will not work. At the same time, if the essence you choose has no effect on you that you can gradually notice, it is not the one your body, mind, and spirit requires for healing to take place. The awesome thing about flower essences is that if they are not needed and ineffective in the body, they quietly dissipate without harm. This is one of things I absolutely love about this therapy—beautiful healing with no side effects!

Flower Essences Therapy

Flower essences are available by drop, spray, cream, and lozenge. You can create your own lotions to apply directly to the skin by simply adding drops to your favorite body lotion. As you learn about the effects of each flower essence, trust your inner voice to guide you to the one that is right for you. Try to introduce one essence at a time so you can evaluate whether it is working for you. If the essence isn't working, it may be because you need to reflect deeper on what healing you are looking for and re-choose an essence. You are the one who knows which essence is right for you. Once you are good at listening to your inner voice, you will be more accurate.

Try these methods of use:

- **REAL Beautiful drinks:** Dispense a couple drops of the flower essence(s) of your own intuitive choice into pure mineral water or any drink you choose. Reflect on the healing you want to take place as you mindfully sip your drink to help boost the power and effects.

- **On or under tongue:** Place a couple of drops of your chosen flower essence on or under your tongue. Try your best to allow time for the essence to infiltrate your being by not eating at the same time.

- **Add to your bath:** Add flower essence to your bathwater to allow the energy of the essence to penetrate into your body cells and have its effect while you breathe deeply and rest.

- **Rub or dab gently onto skin:** Because our skin has pores, everything you put on it has a vibrational impact on every cell within. The flower essences that heal emotional wounds inside can also heal physical wounds on your body. Scratches, scars, infections, and pain can all be soothed with the application of flower essences directly on the area of injury or discomfort.

Secret Magic Potions

(for Trauma, Grief, Fear, Depression, Confidence, Self-Love, Eating Disorders, Stress, Anxiety, Weight Balance, Weight Loss, Addictions, Anger, and MORE)!

Remember that we are vibrating energy and everything outside of us carries a vibration, just as flowers and their essences do. Similar to aromatherapy, flowers offer a natural alternative to ease suffering and bring harmony to the balance of energy inside the mind, body, and spirit when we choose to attend to any emotional concerns we have in life.

My all-time favorite flower essence is Star-of-Bethlehem. I believe every person who begins flower-essence therapy should start with this one. Like a magic potion, Star-of-Bethlehem is a gentle, soothing, and comforting essence that heals you from the inside out. We have all experienced traumas that linger and leave imprints in the cells of the body even when we spend some time embracing, reflecting, and healing from the experience. I decided to use Star-of-Bethlehem to begin my own healing from some of my own life traumas. This beautiful essence provided the awareness and comfort I needed to allow the residual lower levels of energy inside my body to leave.

It is a magical process. I cannot tell you how it all works, but you will feel the change happening if you take the time to make this therapy a daily practice you hold with some reflective and meditative intention. In times when your need to be soothed escalates, keep this essence by your side all day long. From the little hurts that add up on a daily basis in our lives, to larger traumas such as grief, and sexual abuse, let this beautiful remedy remove the pain and heal your soul. This flower essence is the most loving, comforting, healing, and meaningful one I have experienced. As with all flower essences, be listening and observing the messages your mind, body, and spirit shares with you. You may even be surprised to find out about a trauma you had no idea happened to you in your past.

Other Flower Essence Suggestions:

Listen to your intuition and choose the flower essence that you feel called to take.

- **Aspen:** This essence tackles free-floating, nonspecific, or vague fear.

- **Cherry Plum:** This essence is used to balance extremes in emotion or behaviors connected to depression, suicide, compulsions, self-destructive addictions, and abusive thoughts, feelings, or behaviors. The fear of losing control can be connected to many imbalances faced in daily living. This beautiful essence helps to soothe and calm fears that drive us to extremes.

- ***Chestnut Bud:*** If you are unable to stop repeating hurtful patterns, this flower essence is the one of choice. You will feel empowered and gain insight on how to overcome negative patterns to support more optimum experiences in life. Chestnut bud is a hopeful resource for those struggling with disordered eating, addictions, and obsessive-compulsive disorders (OCD) that lower our health and well-being. Chestnut bud is a direct flower-essence therapy for eating disorders. It's also useful for people who suffer from denial and other symptoms of addiction. Like the other chestnut remedies (red chestnut and white chestnut), it is used by flower-essence practitioners to treat any obsessive-compulsive behavior. It is said to help free the individual from compulsions, such as eating when facing an uncomfortable situation.

- ***Clematis:*** This essence helps us to be effective in the moment and get done what is required to make our lives successful and meaningful.

- ***Crab Apple:*** This essence is for self-love. It helps individuals who dislike some part of who they are (personality, a body part). It is also a cleanser and therefore cleanses wounds in body, mind, and spirit. It washes away repetitive or obsessive behaviors that are not healthy. This flower essence is one of a trio that support disordered eating (along with cherry plum and chestnut bud), addictions, and negative ways of living and being. This essence also supports weight loss because of its balancing and cleansing effects.

- **Impatiens**: This essence calms frustration, irritability, and impatience as it helps us to be more relaxed around others.

- **Larch**: For those who lack self-confidence and believe they will not succeed, this essence provides the motivation to take risks and become more involved in life.

- **Mimulus**: For overcoming an identifiable everyday fear—such as public speaking, illness, or pain—mimulus provides courage.

- **Mustard**: This essence lifts depression, relieves hopelessness, and brings peace and joy back into our lives.

- **Olive**: For those suffering from long-term stress, causing tiredness or exhaustion, olive restores mental and physical strength and provides faith to move forward beyond stressful circumstances.

- **Red Chestnut**: I love this essence for mothers. Our natural and innate instinct to protect our loved ones can cause us to be overprotective at times. This comforting essence releases the tension and stress our way of being causes. It encourages a sense of calm energy that flows through us out to those we love.

- **Rock Rose**: For those who experience fear or terror, this remedy calms us and gives us courage.

- **Star-of-Bethlehem**: This important essence has the power to heal pain, trauma, grief, and hurt in the past and in the present. Allow these negative or painful experiences to be gently removed from your body, mind, and spirit. This flower essence provides REAL Beautiful comfort.

- **Sweet Chestnut**: When there seems to be no light at the end of the tunnel, sweet chestnut cures our sense of hopelessness and despair. It renews our spirit; new opportunities open up, and life begins to magically flow.

- **White Chestnut**: This essence can help women who have repetitive negative self-evaluations. It stops negative mind chatter or mind torture that inhibits our ability to think clearly and feel at peace. Halting these thoughts can undo the damage and remove the neural pathways that make women feel unworthy and "not good enough."

Flower Essence Remedies

Remedies combine different flower essences to re-pattern, unblock, and bring harmony and balance to the energy systems within. Find a combination using the essences described above to help you in specific life struggles.

Disordered Eating, Addictions, and Obsessive-Compulsive Disorders

Combine the following essences:
- chestnut bud
- crab apple
- cherry plum

Self-Love and Empowerment

Combine the following essences:
- crab apple
- larch

Stress and Burnout

Rescue Remedy is a power-packed combination of five essences in one that helps to calm and soothe the nerves and heal the tired body, mind, and spirit. It's a great way to alter the vibration inside your body cells to raise them so you can find inner peace and bliss.

Combine the following essences:

- rock rose

- impatiens

- clematis

- star-of-bethlehem

- cherry plum

Fear

Combine the following essences:

- mimulus

- rock rose

- aspen

Repetitive Thoughts and Mental Anguish

Combine the following essences:

- white chestnut

- sweet chestnut

Bailey Flower Essences

As related at the beginning of this discussion, Arthur Bailey loved and believed in Dr. Bach's discoveries and felt called to go even deeper to intuitively create more flower-essence remedies, expanding the choices of remedies to cover those emotional aspects untouched in Bach's remedies. Bailey closed the gap for those who suffer, using many intelligent composite remedies to reach and heal some very significant emotional concerns. I will list some of his combination essences that I feel are helpful to all women.

- **Anger and Frustration:** brings harmony and balance to our energy so we can properly manage our lives

- **Fears:** helps to dissipate fear so no restrictions exist

- **Self-Esteem:** brings forth a sense of empowerment

- **Liberation:** for those who get stuck and overpowered by other people's energy

- **Depression and Despair:** unlocks negative patterns connected to despair

- **Tranquility:** empowers as it centers us in the now and brings peace and calm to the mind

- **Sadness and Loneliness:** provides comfort, love, and assurance

- **Childhood:** unblocks and frees energy locked inside since childhood

- **Grief:** soothes all types of grief and anguish

- **Confusion:** helps us to see clearly

- **Shock and Trauma:** soothes us when we feel shaken or devastated

- **Stuck-in-a-Rut:** unblocks the circumstances that make us feel trapped

These blends are available at The Great Vine, 36 Main Street East, Huntsville Ontario, P1H 2C8. Call them at 1-705-789-3737 and give them your order. They will deliver this wonderful therapy to your door.

Please search for flower essence remedies available throughout Canada, the United States and across the world.

Chapter 15

Sacred Sadhana

*The sacred and spiritual experience is said to have no place in science,
yet to fully know and appreciate life and our place in it,
I believe both dimensions need to be present.*
—Sondra Barrett, Ph., D.

Enlightened Master of Our Time: Dr. Rangie Singh

I HAVE HAD MANY MAGICAL AND synchronistic moments while writing this book. Every one of them was a beautiful message from the divine universal power reminding me of the magic in the content I was including in this book and to guide me further in the writing of it. One such divine connection was the one I experienced with Dr. Ranjie Singh.

On two occasions when I met with Dr. Singh, he revealed secrets to me that I believe bring the power of all of the insights, practices, and technologies in this book to higher, more potent, and more sacred levels. Dr. Singh's book, *Self-Healing: Powerful Techniques*, was mystically handed to me while I was waiting for my healing mantra cards to be printed in a print shop one day—a shop I intuitively picked because it was the first one to show up in my Internet search even though it was inconveniently on the other side of the city. The book was shown to me as an example of the book-printing ability of this particular print shop, but it was the research discussed inside the book and the fact that the researcher himself lived in my city, that caught my eye. The contents of the book gave further credibility to many of the concepts I was sharing in this book— energy vibration, mantras, sounds, visualization, meditation, breath/ *pranayama*, higher consciousness, and how the pineal gland connects us to better health and higher divine consciousness (a very large part of the Kundalini Yoga technology shared further on in this book). Dr. Singh unknowingly shared some divine secrets with me in the two separate meetings I had with him.

Deeper Than "The Secret"

When I walked into Dr. Singh's office on the day of my first appointment, I was overwhelmed, in a spiritual way, by his presence. This feeling or high-energy tingling happens when two higher energies are mixing or a high energy impacts a lower one. Dr. Singh told me himself it is very unusual for him to meet up with people in this way, but that, being intuitive himself, he followed his own inner knowing that told him to meet me.

We talked about my interest in his research, and I told him about my book. Our discussions surrounded the topic of energy, healing, and his research, which led me to share with him my near-death experience. Dr. Singh told me that when higher levels of emotion are induced, a spiritual experience can take place, such as connection to spirit and higher vibrational levels of energy. This insight became the first part of a critical ingredient that empowers the energy practices and technologies I share throughout this book. As we learned from Gregg Braden in chapter 12, emotions carry the feelings that speak the language of the universe. Dr. Singh stated that the highly intense emotions I felt during my severe illness likely played a role in my near-death experience, as research has uncovered.

The second secret insight he shared as an aside while relating findings from his research connected to his book. Dr. Singh noted that honor/reverence must be present in the application of the techniques and therapies cited in his research. I had another spine-tingling spirit-connected moment, and I felt divinely guided to know that creating emotions that contain reverence within them uplift the power in all of the insights, practices, and technologies in this book to the highest and most sacred levels. The levels where the highest power of the universe reigns and magic and miracles live!

The Secret of All Secrets

The Secret Power Behind Honor and Reverence

Although the words honor and reverence, and the feelings they would conjure inside are similar (high regard and respect reserved for things held sacred and divine); the meaning behind the word or act of '*honor*' also includes *a sense of worthiness and love*. I felt guided to add the word honor alongside the word reverence to capture the greatest understanding of the meaning and emotion I am trying to guide you to uphold when you add this *secret of all secrets* to all of your future energy raising practices or *sacred sadhana*, as I will teach you in this chapter. I took these two insights and combined them with the teachings of Gregg Braden regarding the power in our thoughts and emotions to create the feelings that communicate to the field of energy inside and around us to manifest the reflection of these. If our emotions carry the vibration honor and reverence hold, they create feelings that speak directly to the highest power in the divine field of energy in the universe that also contains heaven. This insight could explain my visit in heaven with my grandmother. All of the right magical ingredients were present: the intensely focused emotional energy brought on by my illness, the feelings of belief and honor I held inside when I asked my grandmother to show heaven to me, mixed with the highest level of reverence in the moment when I sacredly honored her life and kissed her good-bye on the day of her funeral.

Sparkling Insight

So the secret of all secrets that reaches depths deeper than 'The Secret' itself, involves adding the emotion of the greatest and most sacred honor and reverence you can manage to every practice, along with the other important things I have told you (focused intention and attention, high energy words, sacred insights, the science behind beauty and miracles, stillness, listening, observing, reflection, and so on). If we make our living and being and every energy practice we choose to include in our lives sacred; we expedite the experience of magic and miracles, and heaven too!

Sacred Sadhana

To take part in practices that become sacred, we must feel honor and reverence at high levels. Thus we need to create this high intensity emotion inside us with consistency to make the magical power it contains manifest. I call this powerful practice *Sacred Sadhana*. The path to all of your desires unfolds when you choose to add this approach to your living and being in your daily life. To help you create a *sacred sadhana*, listen in on the beautiful secrets that follow.

In her book *The Path of Practice: A Woman's Book of Ayurvedic Healing*, Maya Tiwari explains that "*sadhana* is a Sanskrit word whose root, *sadh*, means to reclaim that which is divine within us, our power to heal, serve, rejoice, and uplift the spirit. *Sadhana* practices encompass all our daily activities, from the simple to the sublime—from cooking a meal to exploring your inner self through meditation." It is obvious by now that if we want to stay connected to higher levels of vibrational energy that link us to our highest being, power and experiences in life, we have to commit to spending time in daily practices that keep our vibrational energy high. But we also have to become saturated in these practices with a vibration that remains inside all day long. We add in and become the vibration that is contained in the meaning behind the words *honor* and *reverence*, and then miracles are sent to us uninterrupted. We have to fill our days with these sacred vibrations. This means there is some work involved, but the rewards are priceless.

I have come to crave my own *sacred sadhana*, for it feeds me in ways nothing else in my life has ever been able to do. I have also come to love the word *sadhana* and all that it means, because understanding it has dramatically changed my life in truly miraculous ways. Of course, to do what is required demands our time. I know what you are saying: "Where is the time in our crazy hectic schedules to add this stuff in?" My answer is, *everywhere*.

Sparkling Insight

When you set aside time to take part in sacred sadhana you are given the beautiful gift of expanding time. It is another energy secret and a miraculous thing to watch unfold. Like magic, time expands in response to your dedication to take part in sacred sadhana and appointments will be suddenly canceled, your energy will be increased, you'll feel unusually inspired, time will go by slowly, and you'll feel as if you are in a time warp that allows you to slow your life down, get your work done more effectively, and fit in more energy-raising practices/sadhana.

When I witness time expanding in my own life, it makes me smile. This is just another fun magic-wand waving activity you can try out for yourself. It is a powerful experience that you have to feel to believe. You have to trust me and the countless other people across the world that know this works—take the chance and try it. Get committed to a daily sadhana with your best effort to make it happen, and then experience the magic. Not only will time expand, other magical things will take place too.

Making It Sacred

The phrase *'sacred sadhana'* and the inspiration for this chapter came to me one day while I was completely immersed in sadhana. I could actually feel my body vibrating. It was a magical moment, similar to many others that surround me because of the technologies I have practiced and shared in this book. It highlighted the extreme power of the focus I had gained while lost in the energy-raising practice I was applying, along with the energy of the feelings of honor and reverence I held inside the cells of my body. I became one with the highest vibration in the universe and could feel this vibration alive inside of me. This experience was another one of the many miracles that happened to me while lost in the insights and practices I was studying. In this case, I was listening to scientific and sacred music that helped to create a vibration inside my body, while reciting one of my favorite healing mantra meditations. All of the efforts I made to increase the vibrational energy inside of me through *sacred sadhana,* brought me to this sacred level. I have included a list of the things I do to make my sadhana sacred below. The synergistic power of all of these things combined is greater than the sum of their individual energies.

Sparkling Insight

When you combine many energy-raising practices together and add honor and reverence from your heart to them; sacred sadhana happens. If you make your sadhana sacred, you become linked to the higher vibrational energy from which magic and miracles are created.

The information I share with you in this book helps you learn many individual energy-raising practices at a time, and then ends with a technology that combines many into one. I did this intentionally because I think you have to incorporate and become knowledgeable in each practice individually, and then over time you can manage putting all of them together in an effective way. Step by step, your life becomes immersed in these powerful energy-raising vibrations, and the miracles shower down like a million raindrops—completely beautiful. It is the vibration that you carry within you that can make this happen if it is constructed properly.

All of this insight brings us to the ways of creating *sacred sadhana*. We simply infuse our high-energy practice with honor and reverence. Every high-energy practice you incorporate in your sadhana has power, but be sure to make the time you set aside worth your effort.

The Ways to Sacred Sadhana

- Above all things, you need to saturate your being and energy practices with honor and reverence (practice becoming the feeling of honor and reverence).

- Include as many energy-raising items, practices and technologies as you can to boost your practice to higher levels of energy more quickly. Alongside the specific practice or technology of your choice, choose some of the following things to elevate the energy in the sacred space you create; vibrational music, healing incense, medicinal herbs, high-energy photos, aromatherapy with essential oils, stones, symbols, and anything that you feel called to include. Practice in the sun, outside in nature, so that you can draw in energy from all of these sources of high energy, and choose the practices you would like to incorporate into a special sadhana just for you.

- Be consistent. Consistency contains the power of many angels as Yogi Bhajan will inform you in a quote a little further on in the book.

- Remember that the time you spend in sadhana pays you back

in many priceless ways, one being that it expands time for you and the other being it nudges the unseen forces in and around you to come to your aid and make magic happen.

- Taking part in sadhana that includes the information in this book will impart magic and miracles in your life.

- All possibilities are open when you practice *sacred sadhana* and guide it to an intention that you stay focused on—peace, healing, bliss, weight loss, success, prosperity … anything you want!

- Believe in the impossible. It is part of what makes dreams and wishes come true.

- Keep the golden connection to your spirit alive, for it is the only way to the highest power where higher consciousness (divine intuition) exists. Being connected to the spirit part of you by uplifting your vibrational energy has to happen to reach living and being REAL Beautiful.

A Sacred Secret

Take part in *sacred sadhana* in the "ambrosial hours"…learn more about this beautiful secret in the sparkling insight below.

Sparkling Insight

If we take advantage of the secrets Rumi is trying to share with us in the clever poem that follows, we learn that the "ambrosial hours," about two and a half hours before sunrise, have some secrets hidden and waiting for us to discover if we are willing. The powerful angle of the sun, the quiet and undisturbed peacefulness, and the potent levels of the life force we breathe in have the power to skyrocket the effects of any meditation and sadhana to sacred levels. I believe these precious hours hold the key to open the door Rumi refers to where the connection to highest knowing, highest power, heaven and the veils between worlds meet.

> *The breeze at dawn has secrets to tell you.*
> *Don't go back to sleep.*
> *You must ask for what you really want.*
> *Don't go back to sleep.*
> *People are going back and forth across the doorsill*
> *Where the two worlds touch.*
> *The door is round and open.*
> *Don't go back to sleep.*
> *—Rumi*

It is with much gratitude that I thank Dr. Rangie Singh for his critical research that contains the power to uplift us all to higher energy dimensions.

Chapter 16

The Voice Inside

There is a voice inside which speaks and says:
"This is the real me."
—William James

Listening

*I*N THESE FAST-PACED AND STRESSFUL times, we often ignore the things we know deep inside we should be doing and being. We dance around and put our time and focus into everything but the things we know in our heart that we should choose first. There is a voice inside that prods us, reminds us, begs our attention, but we just don't listen.

Psychologist William James enlightens us with his expert wisdom in the quote that opens this chapter to remind us of the knower, the knowing, and the truth within us. Let's listen better to the guide inside that teaches us and lights the pathway to our higher self and highest power.

REAL Beautiful Gift #8
Insights from *Real Magic* by Dr. Wayne Dyer

"Spiritual people know, by virtue of having been there and experienced it firsthand, that one can get divine guidance by becoming peaceful and quiet and asking for answers."

I have come to know and honor the voice inside that guides me, protects me, and answers every question I have. Like you, I have had many moments in life when I have ignored this voice out of confusion, unconsciousness knowing, and because of the busyness of life surrounding me. Because of this, I missed out on the infinite insight it was trying to give me. Many spiritual masters tell us to look inside or within for the untold secrets that rest there. Too many times I have silenced this voice, not realizing the treasures hidden in its divine wisdom. I cut myself off from the frequency and the gifts it was trying to guide me towards instead of tapping into it, as I do now. You too are connected to this mystical intelligence, whether you know it or not, whether you believe it or not. As I have studied and researched the wisdom of many health experts and healing masters, I have been exposed to a universal truth that lives and breathes inside of us. If you listen closely, you too can hear the secrets this voice will share with you and take advantage of its power. This entity, consistent and faithful, infinite and real, never leaves your side, never wavers in truth and wisdom. Even in our most valiant attempts to lose it, destroy it, or deny it; it remains.

This voice I speak of is the infinite and undying part of the true being that we can access while we are alive, and it will live on even after our physical bodies die. Countless spiritual masters teach us to listen to this divine intelligence. They are sharing little brilliant gems of knowledge gleaned from their research and hours of long study. Open your mind and think outside the box as I take you on a journey to know the things you don't even know you don't know, about who you really are.

Listening Closer

As your journey to a deeper self-understanding of the mind, body, and spirit continues, I want you to become familiar with the voice inside you. The one you hear talking incessantly at times and conclude, on most occasions, to be nothing but mindless chatter. I am asking you to begin a reconnection to this inner voice and start listening more closely to what it is saying. The voice could sound just like you, a friend, or even a loved one that has passed on. Maybe it is the voice of a spirit guide or angel? Once you hear the voice, I want you to go a step further and ask the voice a question. Maybe you ask the voice if you should change jobs, or let go of a relationship; maybe you want to know the truth about something that confuses you or ask for financial help, healing or peace. Go ahead, just ask.

Once you ask your question, I want you to let the question go as if it was a note left inside a helium balloon that has just taken flight into the sky toward the mystical universe that surrounds each and every one of us. Tell the universe you will wait for the answer to your question. I know this may feel a little strange at first, but trust me, as we go along, you will have regular conversations with yourself and the universe at the same time, you will honor it, and you will know the power of it too. For now, just let the question go and wait for your answer.

Go forward with your plans for the day with a consciousness and awareness that the question is out there and belive that an answer will come back to you. If you keep this expectation in your mind and keep your level of awareness up so that you can hear the answer when it comes, you will know when the answer has been given. I see this exercise as one of my favorite ways to link to the miracles that exist in life. Every time I receive an answer, it feels just like magic to me.

Once you let go of your question to the universe, you need to start paying attention to the people you meet, the information people give you, the phone calls that reach you, the mail in the mailbox, the e-mails you receive, the billboard signs on the highway, the songs that play on the radio, the opportunities that present themselves to you, the message the little old lady you bump into at the grocery store shares with you, and any way that an answer could be delivered to you via information streams. The answer might be revealed directly by your own voice inside or indirectly through another information source. You yourself will know when the answer arrives by the mystical connection you will feel to it.

I believe that when you sit quiet and in honor of this voice, you begin a divine journey back to health and empowerment in your mind, body, and spirit. That muted voice inside you is all-knowing and connected to a universal energy that has the power to heal and uplift you to a vibration level of being unknown to many, but available to all. All you have to do is ask for guidance from it, and it will answer you back. This practiced skill is required to bring you to deeper understanding of your energy being.

We will learn more about this truth as you move forward in the book. For right now, I need you to let go and trust for a while with a willingness to listen and believe in a wisdom that exists in and outside of you—powerful beyond your imagination—but only if you are willing.

Everything in the universe is within you. Ask all from yourself.
—Rumi

Your Inner Voice—The Process

I have tried to simplify the connection to your inner voice in the steps that follow. Just like a trusted guide, the universe will send an answer to you from its intelligence, and your infinite voice inside will whisper the answer to you if you are ready to listen.

Listen and observe while you note the ways in which this voice responds back to you. I promise you will begin to experience and know this mystical and magical power in and around you. With practice, it becomes like your own personal GPS that will faithfully guide you in life toward anything you desire.

1. Close your eyes and sit in a quiet, comfortable, and peaceful place.

2. Take three full and deep breaths, in and out through the nose.

3. Allow the sights and sounds that surround you to be, as you embrace them and allow them to pass through you.

4. Observe the sounds, words, and messages you are hearing and gently acknowledge them.

5. What is the voice inside saying?

6. Take the knowledge that is being shared with you and reflect on it, even if the message is telling you something you don't want to hear, for example, "You are full of anger or anxiety." If this is the message you hear, then you need to listen and ask, "Why am I angry or anxious?"

7. When you receive your answer, take action in the real world to decrease your anger or anxiety. Ask the universe for help in doing this. It is the quickest way to suggestions that really work. You will be surprised at how effortlessly you can resolve lifelong issues when you listen to the insight downloaded to you from this divine source of intelligence within you.

8. Continue to go inside to listen to see what other wisdom your inner voice shares with you on a daily basis. Ask for guidance to address any concerns, questions, or confusion you might be having. Always ask this inner wisdom to guide you to the resources required to help resolve, support, or enhance the wisdom shared. Act upon this guidance in the real world.

9. Repeat the process above and tailor it to the support and guidance you most require. The responses are like magic because when we listen to our inner voice, it guides us to healing, peace, bliss, success, abundance, and even magic

and miracles if we request it with devotion in our hearts. Trust your instincts to identify the answer when it comes, in whatever way it chooses to be revealed to you, and listen to your inner voice for the final answer in the end. Take note of the transformations that will happen one after another to unfold the pathway to the resources you need and the answers you seek. Just like magic, they will appear.

What inspires you? What are you naturally good at? What do you know deep in your own soul? What do you gravitate toward? What makes you feel good and empowered? If you could do or be anything you wanted, what would it be? What do you like? What do you not like? What part of you hides inside that you know is "really you" but are afraid to express because you fear being mocked, judged, or silenced if you become it? The universe understands only truth. When we speak truth, live it, and become it, magical things happen. When you reflect on these questions and start answering them honestly, you are on your way to living an authentic life—and then, the universe comes to you with its magic.

Chapter 17

The Miracles in Our Breath

*Inhale and God approaches you. Hold the inhalation and
God remains with you. Exhale and you approach God.
Hold the exhalation, and surrender to God.*
—Sri Tirumalai Krishnamacharya

The Science Behind Our Breath

*O*UR BREATH IS THE CARRIER of the *life force* we bring into the body through inhalation and exhalation caused by the diaphragm. "One complete breath" is defined as the sequence and completion of one respiratory inhalation followed by one exhalation. Pranayam is the scientific control of the movement of prana (*an upward current of energy in the body containing life force*), and apana (*a downward current of energy that forms in the body and removes the waste products and all that we don't need from the body*). As we take this life containing essence into our lungs, it breathes it into every cell in the body. As we inhale, it forms a sacred and mystical current of energy inside the body that contains all of the secret elements of life.

Sparkling Insights

There are secrets hidden in the way we breathe. When we inhale prana through the nose, it directly activates the pineal gland or third eye (Ajna) inside the brain. The activation of this one tiny gland creates a beautiful cascade effect as it signals the function of the master gland or hypothalamus, which in turn masterfully guides the function of all other endocrine glands in the body (pituitary, thyroid, parathyroid, adrenals, reproductive organs, and the pancreas), and the release of melatonin (a health tonic for the body, insomnia, depression, cancer, higher consciousness, and more), as related in Dr. Ranjie Singh's research and book, Self-Healing Techniques, described in chapter 15.

Ayurvedic and yogic physician Sri Tirumalai Krishnamacharya eloquently expressed the great power our own breath contains in the quote that introduces this chapter. It is powerful to know that when we breathe, we are taking in God (the divine source) or the highest energy of the universe. As we have learned from science, research, and enlightened and spiritual masters across time, this golden elixir is steeped with much more than just oxygen as its sole ingredient, as it is so often simplified when described. That our bodies have the ability to mechanically breathe and draw this life force into it, is a miracle in itself.

Without our breath and the prana within it, life as we know it would cease to exist. This truth alone should cause us to honor and revere it. So often, though, we take our breath for granted because of its automatic nature. Some of us still do not even comprehend the mystery and magic behind its full potential and power in our lives. I share this chapter to shine light onto the truth and beautiful power our breath holds so that our gratitude and honor for it will be uplifted.

As we shift into another level of consciousness every night when we go to sleep, what is it that keeps our breath working for us? Dr. Wayne Dyer calls it "the ghost in the machine." I became intrigued by this essence or ghost when I studied anatomy and physiology and was astounded at the miraculous array of functions—both automatic and controlled by us—going on inside of me that I never knew existed. All of these functions were unseen and hidden from my view as they are from yours. These beautiful secrets sat inside me, as they do you, unknown until further depths were uncovered. I felt like I had entered another world when I became aware of the inner workings of our anatomy and physiology.

When I lay sick with pneumonia, propped up with pillows on the arm of the leather couch I rested on for over six weeks just to breathe easier, in the quiet darkness of the night while I lay awake unable to sleep, I experienced this mysterious force take charge of my breath for me. It moved my breath for me as it forcefully filled my lungs with prana and then exhaled in its own timing. This rather forceful inhalation and exhalation played out for several breaths, as I became the observer of this invisible intelligence that knew more about what I needed than I did. I witnessed this secret and sacred essence inside my body breathe for me when I couldn't, as it seemed to know I needed more oxygen and life force, even when I didn't.

I was both frightened and intrigued to experience the presence of this intangible ghost; I can only describe it as miraculous and divine in nature. It was this event, along with my near-death experience, and all of the miracles and masterful insights I have come to know beyond the miracles behind our breath, that have helped me to understand the great power and beauty that lives inside who I really am. If we breathe in and out more consciously in our daily lives, we will not only uncover the secrets behind the power of our breath; we will open the gates to heaven where a flood of divine vibrations/miracles—peace, bliss, abundance, higher consciousness, and more—are waiting to be expressed. In the stressful and imbalanced pace we keep every day, if our breath is stifled, we are robbed of the pure joy of living that our physical body is capable of creating for us.

Don't forget the power and the pharmacy that lives inside the physical body that we already discovered in chapter 5, and how we can increase our vibrational energy with every thought we hold, by saturating ourselves and others with beauty, forgiveness, blessings, love, honor, reverence, peace, kindness, truth, giving, receiving, and feelings that uplift our vibrations—and now, by the way we breath. We are energy beings who can make our own magic potions. It is up to you to learn and incorporate the practices and technologies that can do this.

If our breath contains God or the highest power of the universe that brings everything we intend to us, then everything we need is in our breath. If we raise our vibrations, we connect with the gifts available. Otherwise, we are at risk for lower energies like stress, fear, scarcity, anxiety, depression, anger, body imbalances, and narrow negative perspectives that will override the higher vibrations. Shallow and unconscious breathing blocks the door to REAL Beautiful living and being. It cuts off our communication to the divine universal intelligence that holds the magic of life itself within it. It makes sense, then, that we should breathe better, longer, deeper, and with more honor and reverence. As Yogi Bhajan teaches us in the knowledge shared in chapter 19 of this book, when we breathe consciously instead of unconsciously, the universe will reach out to us.

The Secrets in Our Breath

The diaphragm, which enables our breathing, is sometimes called our "second heart," according to Dr. Dharma Singh Khalsa in his book *Meditation as Medicine: Activate the Power of Your Natural Healing Force.* It is a secret gateway to immunity, health, healing, peace, a calm and balanced nervous system, the release of anger, fear, and pain, as well as a way to the bliss we all search for in life. This powerful knowledge once again reminds us of the miraculous beings we are. Every system, organ, tissue, cell, molecule, atom, subatomic particle, and space within us can be filled with the life force that brings all these good things to us when we use the gifts we have been given inside our physical bodies and our ability to breathe and take in life force.

Since breath is so often taken for granted, we miss the magic power it holds unless we consciously choose to insert breath practice into our lives. Yogis become so efficient in breathing, because of the dedicated time and practice they put into it, that they can direct the flow of prana to any organ or area in the body they choose. They also receive a constant download of divine insights and miracles. This same ability can connect anyone dedicated to *pranayama* to become one with the highest and most divine vibrations in the universe.

In *The Hindu Yogi Science of Breath,* authors William Walker Atkinson and Lon Milo Duquette explain that the yogi "knows something about 'prana,' of which his Western brother is ignorant, and he is fully aware of the nature and manner of handling that great principle of energy, and is fully informed as to its effect upon the human body and mind. He knows that by rhythmical breathing one may bring himself into harmonious vibration with nature, and aid in the unfoldment of his latent powers."

The ancient yogis discovered that the secret of Cosmic Consciousness is intimately linked with breath mastery.
—*Gyanavatar Swami Sri Yukteswar Giriji*

Just Breathe...

There is peace in every breath.
—*Snatam Kaur*

As Snatam Kaur mentions in the quote above, one of the gifts breathing practice brings is inner peace. Prana dissolves the chemical reactions in our bodies that create anxiety, fear, and all nervous tension. When we use our breath to stop the release of these harmful chemicals, we create the chemistry that uplifts our mood and brings peace to the mind, body, and spirit instead. Additional miracles behind our breath in general include the following:

Disease never lives in a well-oxygenated body.
—*Donna Eden*

- increased immunity and ability to prevent colds, respiratory infections, and illness throughout the body

- improved energy, vitality, radiance, and beauty in the physical body

- exercise for internal vital organs, such as the lungs, diaphragm, liver, and intestines, to improve the function of these and every other system in the body

- the delivery of food, nutrients, blood, oxygen, and the essence of breath—universal vital cosmic energy—to every cell in the body

- elevated consciousness so that we can receive divine knowledge and intelligence

- survival for every cell in the body

- movement and release of toxins throughout the entire body

- breakdown of fat molecules by the oxygen in breath

- increase of metabolism through full, deep breaths

- boosted immunity to protect the body from illness

- calm for our nerves through balancing of the sympathetic and parasympathetic nervous systems

- reduction in addictive impulses

- synchronization of the biorhythms of the body

- strengthening of the nervous system to protect us from stress

- circulation to every cell in the body, raising each to its optimum function

- increased level of vibration connecting the body to all similar vibrations—health, self-love, healing, peace, bliss, and so on

- released anxiety and depression

- connection to the spirit part of our being outside of our physicality

- better functioning of the brain and clearer thinking

- slowed rates of breath that encourage meditative states, a connection to divine consciousness that causes enlightenment and the experience of samadhi, or oneness with the universe

*Take a minute and reflect on how you breathe from moment
to moment—the rhythm of your breath reflects your life.*

The Secrets in Slowing Down Our Breath

The rate, depth, and rhythm of our breath determine the state of our mind and health. If we can slow, deepen, and balance the rhythm, we can increase the opportunity for all of the benefits listed above. The mind and all the cells of the body are listening to the commands of the breath and responding accordingly with health benefits and experiences that mirror each breath.

The secret is to decrease the number of breaths we have in one minute. The greatest achievement would be managing one breath per minute—20-second inhalation, 20-second retention, 20-second exhalation. Below, I have described some powerful breath exercises that you can incorporate into a daily *sacred sadhana* to invite optimal health and miracles into your life.

Secret Breath Practices

The Complete Breath or the Three-Part Yogic Breath

The complete yogic breath involves expanding the lungs and reaching all spaces within them: upper, middle, and lower lobes or areas of the lung. Inhale and allow your abdomen to expand while you fill your lungs from the bottom to the top. Once you do this, hold on to the breath as long as you can without creating any pressure inside you. With practice, you will be able to retain the breath for a longer period of time.

Sparkling Insight

To retain breath longer at the end of inhalation, when the pressure to exhale takes place, try to inhale a bit more breath or slightly release some to avoid creating a negative pressure inside you. It is in these moments of retention that the elements of life-force can saturate your cells. Follow this same process when you try to sustain exhalation by exhaling more or inhaling to escape the negative pressure once again so you can take advantage of the opportunity to release and detox what you don't need any more. These secrets allow you the greatest benefits from inhaling and exhaling the breath.

The breath exercise that follows is a simple and effective practice that can be done throughout the day to encourage all of the health benefits listed when pranayama becomes a consistent practice, and when oxygen and life force are increased inside the body.

The Eleven-Second Miracle Breath

Practice this breath for eleven minutes daily for 40 days, and write down the positive changes you experience in your life. You will rewire your brain, and adjust the negative patterns of your life so that they vibrate at the level of miracles. The number eleven in numerology is considered a master number, and the vibrational energy within it brings perfect balance and connection to spirit. This breath exercise combines the power of many vibrational secrets. It will lift you up to the place where miracles live! Make it a *sacred sadhana*, and infuse it with all of the things that can expedite your higher vibrational state (see chapter 15).

Be sure to add honor and reverence along with the power of some of the mudras shared in this book (see chapters 9, 13, 19 & 20). I will add the power of a sacred mantra to this exercise as well. A sacred mantra is one that has been intentionally imbued with a vibration chosen by a highly enlightened guru. The combination of the words and sounds in the mantra are like a magic code being unlocked inside the body, as it heals and empowers it in some way, because of its vibration. The vibration, meaning, and essence of these words can become one with our being when recited verbally in a sacred way. This powerful and ancient practice is called *japa,* and is well-known to many spiritual masters, religions, and enlightened people across the world.

1. Sit in a comfortable position that allows your spine to form a straight line with the neck so prana can flow unobstructed.

2. Breathe in through your nose, a deep and full breath that expands your lungs fully for an eleven-second count.

3. Gently retain this breath inside you for eleven seconds (without pressure).

4. As you slowly let go of the breath for an eleven-second count, notice the warm tingle you feel inside your body in the moment you begin to exhale. Catch this warm feeling and send it to a specific place in your body, or all over your body as you continue to release/exhale the breath outside of you. * Optional: practice maintaining the exhalation as long as you can beyond the end of the breath you exhale for eleven more seconds. *Note: (Extending exhalation is not easy and requires much practice. If you choose this option, allow time and practice to get you there as you embrace what you are able to achieve in the moment).*

5. Continue the same sequence (eleven-second inhale, 11-second retention, 11-second exhale, * optional: 11-second sustained exhalation) and when you feel ready, see the breath you take

in as a white glowing and healing light that you can guide to any place in the body you wish to direct it.

6. Once you have mastered adding the above elements to the sequence, repeat this beautiful *Miracle Mantra* that follows silently as you continue the breath steps in #5 to increase the vibrational power overall.

A Miracle Mantra

A sacred Gurbani Mantra: *Ang Sang Wahe Guru.*

Pronounciation: *Ung Sung Whaa Hey Guroo*

Translation: *"The miracle of God (the highest power), and the experience of God (the highest power), is within each and every fiber." This mantra is from Snatam Kaur's album "Heart of the Universe," and creates the vibrations of the highest power (miracles) inside every cell in your body.*

7. Repeat the eleven-second breath sequence (inhale for 11 seconds, see prana flowing as a white glowing light inside you, retain your breath and this light for 11 seconds, release and guide the warm tingle to a place in the body, and exhale for 11 seconds, * optional: retain exhalation for 11 seconds). Repeat the sacred manta silently as you breathe.

8. Continue this sequence for eleven minutes.

More Breathing Secrets...

Our breath alone is free, flexible, and available to us in any moment. Focusing on it alone can become our *sacred sadhana*. When you feel there is nothing left to do, manage your breath and everything will change. If we physiologically change the chemicals inside of us, it is impossible for us not to transform. When we attach our breath to an intended thought—one filled with honor, reverence, and the energy of the feelings we wish to manifest—the direction and power of each breath we take in and release from us greatly expands.

Breathe in, mentally utter the word "Victory," and exhale.
You'll find the strength of a hundred angels behind you.
—Yogi Bhajan

Breathe in miracles and breathe out the doubt you have they exist.
Breathe in love and breathe out fear.
Breathe in gratitude and breathe out taking things for granted.
Breathe in light and breathe out darkness.
Breathe in healing and breathe out illness.
Breathe in success and breathe out failure.
Breathe in love and breathe out hatred.
Breathe in peace and breathe out war.
Breathe in prosperity and breathe out scarcity
Breathe in beauty and become it!

You choose what you will breathe in and out.

The Secrets Hidden in Our Nostrils

If you stop and observe the flow of your breath through your nostrils, you will often identify that you are breathing through one nostril more than the other. Maintaining a balance between the flow of breath in both nostrils brings a certain balance or equilibrium to the mind, body, and spirit. Sometimes we can intentionally choose to breathe more through one nostril over the other to uncover even more secrets that can help us in our time of need.

Sparkling Insight

Left-nostril breathing connects with the ida nadis—the left nostril energy pathway that is connected to the moon's energy and induces a calming effect on the nervous system. Left-nostril breathing can improve insomnia, reduce stress and anxiety, and reduce compulsive eating habits. Right-nostril breathing connects with the pingala nadis—the right nostril energy pathway connected to the sun's energy—and increases our strength, boosts mood, increases overall energy and alertness, and improves concentration and focus. If we lengthen the time we spend inhaling over exhaling, we increase our energy, and if we lengthen the time we exhale in our breathing rhythm, we calm body, mind, and spirit.

Alternate Nostril Breathing

The practice of alternate nostril breathing is called *nadi sodhan*. When we alternate the flow of prana through our nostrils, magic happens! Sit in a comfortable position and make sure your spine and neck stay in a straight line so the flow of breath can move uninhibited—and follow these steps.

1. Preparations: Your index finger and thumb should form a mudra/hand position in the shape of a U surrounding your nose so that your thumb can rest beside and block off the right nostril, and your index finger can rest beside and block off the left nostril, alternately.

2. To begin, inhale fully and deeply through your left nostril while you block off your right nostril with your right thumb.

3. Then, close off your left nostril with your right index finger as you exhale this breath through the right nostril.

4. Inhale through the right nostril while the left nostril remains blocked by right index finger.

5. Then, block off your right nostril with your right thumb while you exhale through your left nostril, then, inhale through your left nostril.

6. Continue the pattern by alternating nostrils after each inhalation.

7. Continue this breathing sequence for three to 11 minutes.

Health Benefits:

- improves whole-brain functioning, thus brings balance to the function of the right and left brain hemispheres

- brings balance to the body's energy

- encourages a sense of well being

- powerfully cleanses the energy pathways or *nadis* from which breath flows through the body

Ujjayi Pranayama (The Victorious Breath)

There are secret powers hidden in our hands when we hold them in specific positions called *mudras*. I will share more about these magical powers in chapter 19. *Surya* or *ravi* mudra brings strength to the nervous system and supports our energy and health in the mind, body, and spirit. That's the position used in the breathing exercise below.

1. Sit in a comfortable position with a straight spine, an open chest, and with your shoulders back.

2. Place your hands palms up in *surya* or *ravi mudra* (thumb and ring finger tips touch while other fingers remain straight).

3. Close your eyes and become aware or conscious of your breath. Don't control it, just feel and observe it.

4. After one minute, with a relaxed open mouth, draw air into your open mouth as you create tension in the Adam's apple area of the throat. The sound you will make, "ahhha," will sound like an ocean wave inside a seashell. As you breathe out, move the tension to the back of the throat and make the same sound. The sound of the ebb and flow of the ocean will reside as you continue to inhale and exhale through the mouth. Breathe in "ahhha"; breathe out "ahhha."

5. Once you master this sound/breath, close your mouth gently, draw this breath, and create this sound in and out from your nose instead. As you draw the breath in through your nose, you will need the tension in the Adam's apple and back of the throat once again to make this happen.

6. Continue this breath for three to 11 minutes.

Health Benefits:
(In combination with the mudra, this meditation is power-packed)
- heals and rejuvenates the mind, body, and spirit
- soothes the nervous system
- relieves insomnia
- alleviates fluid retention
- cleanses the body
- creates a higher consciousness
- allows us to be victorious in life

Chapter 18

The Secrets in Meditation

REAL Beautiful Gift #9
Insights from *Real Magic* by Dr. Wayne Dyer

"Deep within you is a unified field of unlimited possibilities. When you become competent at going to this wondrous place, you will discover a whole new realm of human experience where all things are possible. It is here where real magic takes place and you begin to manifest all you seek in your physical world."

Why Do We Meditate?

WHY DO WE TRY TO carefully select the images, words, ideas, beliefs, emotions, feelings, and knowledge that we should focus on? Why do we do the mudras, the secret mantras, the mind-bending breath practice? Why do we give and receive love, forgive, care, have gratitude, and infuse honor and reverence into every inch of our being? Why do we take time for *sacred sadhana* when our lives are already exploding with too many things to do and not enough time to do them? We do it all to independently rewire, regenerate, renew, recalibrate, and infuse every cell in the body with higher vibrational energy so we can reset the energy systems inside of us to realign ourselves with the highest vibrating source of power in the universe, our most natural state. While in this state, we are in our greatest harmony and tapped into the divine powers that sit and wait for us to access them and share gifts with us, if we are willing to accept them. It is the stress, greed, jealousy, manipulations, competition, hurt, hate, judgment, fear, sorrow, pain, lack of self-love, negative self-talk, or any other energy draining way of living and being you can think of that steals the higher vibrations away from us. I know you have felt your power escape like I have because of these things.

Because we are energy beings, we absorb energy like a sponge from the world around us. Meditative processes are another technology we can apply to undo the damage and confusion our electrical systems take on so they can reset to the normal balance they were designed for. All of the insights, practices, and technologies I share with you bring the movement of energy inside you into a state of equilibrium and higher vibrations. We mediate through consistent and wholehearted meditations—those that increase our vibrations and those in which we sit still and go within to ask our questions, get answers, and recreate our lives—so that we uncover and experience the sparkling and vibrant streams of energy that connect us to our highest self (the spirit part of who we are), our highest power (God, divine source, universe), and the eternal flow of magic and miracles that Dr. Wayne Dyer speaks of in the gift that begins this chapter.

Meditation allows the full experience of our being and our highest power to unfold, and then all the things we intend with our hearts (with honor and reverence) are created when we focus our attention on them through meditation. As you know already, I call this living and being REAL Beautiful.

The Countless Ways to Meditate in Our Daily Lives

- in every *sacred sadhana* we create with honor and reverence in our heart

- in every moment we take to reflect, listen, trust, and let go to a higher power that rules our lives

- when we consciously take higher forms of energy inside our being

- when we consciously release lower energy from our being

- when we are lost in the searching, seeking, and studying to understand the mysteries behind our being

- in every conscious higher thought and word we choose

- in every sacred and scientifically created mantra or sound we listen to, recite silently or chant out loud

- in every conscious action, belief, feeling, and emotion we implement that contains high levels of energy over those that contain lower ones

- in every conscious beautiful idea, prayer, vision, and expectation we believe in

- in every asana and mudra we hold

- in every moment we feel and express deep gratitude

- in every moment we choose love instead of hate, forgiveness instead of resentment, turning the other cheek instead of being vengeful, thinking of the greater good and serving others first before ourselves

- in every moment we release guilt, anger, fear, doubt, and scarcity from our consciousness and love ourselves in return

- in every moment we notice/feel a wave of emotion or a warm waterfall flow through our bodies indicating our connection to higher realms of energy

- in every conscious breath dedicated to becoming one with the infinite power

- when we sit still and quiet so we can hear the voice inside that guides us to know who we really are

- when we activate the voice inside by raising our level of vibration to the level where our spirit, heaven, our highest power, and magic and miracles live

- in the moment we realize the powerful and sacred science behind who we are

Every meaningful meditation counts toward the sum of the total vibration you create. No effort is ever wasted or too small. The value is recorded and stored inside the vibrational waves that exist in and around you. Begin by dedicating even three minutes to one of the ideas in this book for 40 days and you will be meditating. I promise, even an effort the size of a mustard seed that contains the magical ingredients of consistency and comes from the heart, will transform your life.

Maybe you will choose to complete a full yogic breath for three minutes a day for 40 days. Maybe you will repeat the sacred mantra, "I am bountiful, blissful, beautiful, bountiful, blissful, and beautiful I am" for three minutes a day for 40 days and change nothing else. Maybe you will add three vibration-raising practices to your daily life, or more. It is up to you how fast or slow you will go. Even the smallest commitment can lift vibrations and make magic happen. Do the best you can and see this special time as something you do for yourself (your *sacred sadhana*). It will pay you back in priceless ways.

Meditation Secrets

All I am saying is that the peace you are seeking is already inside you,
in the harmonious functioning of the body.
—U. G. Krishnamurti

Sparkling Insight

Just the act of sitting quietly in easy pose with your hands in gyan mudra (the tips of thumbs and index fingers touching each other while other fingers are straight) and closing your eyes as you focus on the area between the eyebrows—the third eye—opens the flow of divine energy into your body and stimulates the pineal gland, which begins its work to calm and balance all of the rhythms of the mind, body, and spirit. This physiological and scientific truth alone prepares us to connect with the secrets that hide inside the higher vibrations that can be awakened within us. When we stop to mediate, we move into the present moment (the now), we become in sync with the powerful waves of the divine and send a message of trust to the universe that all is well. Staying inside these waves keeps our power high.

Sit still in a comfortable position or preferably in easy pose (you can view an illustration of this pose in the next chapter) with your eyes closed while applying any vibrational practice of your choice from this book. Make this a *sacred sadhana* to elevate your internal vibrational energy so you can connect to the *spirit* part of your being and your highest power. Observe the magical changes and sacred secrets that begin to show up.

The Secrets in Visualization

Dr. Wayne Dyer reminds us in the quote that opens this chapter, about the power we own to access the quiet center inside of us when we take the time to sit in quiet meditation and make contact with higher vibrations—the secret inside of us—that can cause magic and miracles to appear in our lives from the ideas, thoughts, images, feelings, emotions, and intentions we send to it. We meditate to raise our vibrations, but we sit still in these higher vibrations to take in the offerings presented to us, and to see the details of the things we intend to manifest while we are in this space as well. Using our eyes to not only see, but to touch, feel, smell, hear, live, and breathe the things we intend during meditation, raises the power of the vibrations we invite into our lives.

REAL Beautiful Gift #10
Insights from *Real Magic* by Dr. Wayne Dyer

"When you have a vision and you act as if that vision were already here, you create not only the necessary expertise, but you literally become your own miracle worker."

When we sit in meditation and go within to connect with our spirit or highest energy—the real truth of our being and our divine eye sight is revealed— don't forget to see in every detail the things you want to call forth from the realms of magic and miracles. While you meditate, create live moving pictures filled with the sounds, colors, textures and aromas that are a part of the visions you have for yourself and your life. Cut out pictures of these visions and place them on a mirror or decorative board so you can hold the details in your mind's eye while you carry out your meditative practices to help them manifest in your physical world. The type of meditation that involves sending real-life images to recreate in the physical world is called *creative or guided visualization*. This technique is well proven in research and in the personal experience of many people ranging from athletes, to monks living in monasteries, and for those overcoming mental and physical illness. Create the pictures of the life you choose, and see it unfold!

We have already learned the power in our thoughts, words, beliefs, emotions, feelings, and so on throughout this book. It makes sense to bring these consciously created visions and desires to life from the place inside of us that can make magic and miracles happen.

Miracle Light Meditation

1. Sit in a comfortable position/easy pose with a straight spine and neck to allow prana to easily pass through you.

2. Recall the *miracle breath* from chapter 17: An eleven-second inhalation, 11-second retention of breath, 11-second exhalation, with an optional: 11-second suspension of the breath.

     Continue this breath sequence throughout the mediation that follows below.

3. Visualize every cell in your body filled with light that sparkles, and that every sparkle shines and connects with the vibrating web of energy that creates miracles.

4. As your cells become transfused with miracle energy, you know that every unfulfilled wish or dream becomes possible at this level of vibration.

5. Increase the intensity of the concentration of the vibration in your body cells as sparks of miracle-infused light surround you on all sides and form a radiating spiral from the top of your head to the ground.

6. You become sealed inside this miracle light, while the self-love, healing, bliss, peace, success, and anything else you choose to intend, becomes manifested.

7. Feel the feeling of miracles in your heart. Create the

excitement and awe that reflect the experience of them when they happen, and believe that they are already here.

8.   Spend some time in this vibration every day to re-infuse your cells so you can maintain the level of vibration that links you to miracles.

Sparkling Insight

Create vivid and clear moving pictures of the miracles you want to manifest in your life. After you set up the sparkling vibration above—fill it with the light, feelings, and the emotions required, and then direct the creation of the reality you desire. Whether your intention is directed to the experiences related in step 6, or on a specific relationship, the healing and health of your physical body, the house you want to live in, the love and beauty you want to illuminate, the abundance you want to enjoy, or the power you want to radiate out to the world—it is up to you! In the moment you feel a warm flood of energy pass through your body just as you begin to exhale your breath, send this energy along with your detailed moving vision out to the universal power to create it in real life for you. Let go of it and believe the physical manifestation is before you when you open your eyes.

9.   Repeat the practice above for forty days and record the results. If all is not fully manifested, continue with the practice until all elements appear in your life. Remember to create your visualization to contain the details of any manifestation of your choice.

Remember that you are the magic and miracle maker who uses the alchemy of your own human design to reach higher vibrations to construct the heaven on earth of your choice. The more you practice energy-raising meditations, the higher and more consistent your vibration becomes. With devotion, your ways of living and being become saturated with meditation and the magical gifts that result.

My life feels like one continuous meditation at times because I have become adept at incorporating meditation practices into most of the moments of my day. My thoughts, visions, and desires show up at an expedited rate, instantaneous in some moments. This is what motivates me to continue to adapt my life to make *sacred sadhana* a high priority on my list of things to accomplish in a day. My ability to create magic and miracles becomes so powerful, I do not even have to sit still and go within at times. I can ask, receive, and create without going inside, because I am already there. This experience comes with devoted practice. I also lose this privilege when I lose the practice and the vibration.

How you choose to meditate is up to you. This book shares a variety of ways. The more moments in a day you spend meditating with devotion, the higher your vibration will be, the tighter your connection to spirit, the clearer the guidance, and the easier the creation of magic and miracles.

Life as a Meditation

I try to incorporate meditation into every waking moment of my day. I complete *pranayama* (breath practice) before I go to sleep at night, when I wake up in the morning, and at regular intervals during the day. It is easy to slip in extra deep full breaths before, during, and after I eat or while I drive, cook, shop, walk, exercise, visit, sit in the sun, and so on. I incorporate healing mantras into all of these activities as well. I send love and healing into the food I make and eat, to the loved ones I pray for, to those who are suffering, and to those people and things I am grateful for.

I visualize in blazing color and intricate detail the things I want to become real in my life. I make each and every one of these meditations a *sacred sadhana* that is guided by whatever present desire or need I have in the moment. If I am drained or stressed, I work at meditations that help to raise my vibrational level higher and release lower vibrational energy from my mind, body, and spirit, so that I can prepare a direct link to my highest power. Once higher energy levels are accomplished, then I will sit still in mediation to ask, receive, or create.

More Beautiful Ways to Meditate

The next chapter uncovers the sacred science of Kundalini Yoga as taught by Yogi Bhajan®. It has been described as fast-paced yoga because of the majestic power it yields as it combines many powerful energy raising technologies into one very sacred practice.

Like a beautiful secret, this science was magically imparted into my life the day I was captured by the sound and the voice in the music that played softly in the background of one of my favorite healing stores, The Love Tree in Huntsville, Ontario. It was the sacred and scientific vibrations within the Kundalini music and Gurbani mantras that gave me healing, peace, higher consciousness, and so much more, that caused me to seek to understand Kundalini Yoga on deeper levels. I have been so captured by its power that I have felt called to become a teacher of this beautiful science. Behold the sparkling jewels Kundalini Yoga offers those who practice it. I share these very special meditations with gratitude, honor and reverence from my heart.

Chapter 19

Enlightened Master of Our Time: Yogi Bhajan

Just be you.
—Yogi Bhajan

In Honor of Yogi Bhajan

J DEDICATE THIS CHAPTER TO YOGI Bhajan: spiritual teacher, master of Kundalini Yoga, Ph. D. in Communications Psychology, author, and peaceful visionary. Yogi Bhajan risked his life to bring Kundalini Yoga as taught by Yogi Bhajan® to us because of the veils of secrecy that surround it that we have already mentioned in this book, and because he knew the Western world needed it the most. He brought Kundalini Yoga to the West from the East specifically to help us manage and survive the Aquarian Age that is now upon us. Yogi Bhajan's higher insight guided him to teach us how to deal with the heightened levels of stress, chaos, illness, and unrest he knew this age would bring. But even beyond this beautiful offering, Yogi Bhajan made it his mission with great passion in his heart, to guide women to know and experience the truth of their birthright; to live a bountiful, blissful, and beautiful life.

Mystical Beauty, Power, Abundance, Magic and Miracles

Like a magic elixir, Yogi Bhajan created a penetrable mantra for women that contained the sacred and scientific vibrations he knew would uplift them to the REAL Beautiful and powerful beings they were born to be. You can access the mystical mantra on my website @ www.realbeauitful.ca. It is a unique and beautiful gift you can share with all of the women you love, at healing conferences/retreats, or at any venue while you stand by and observe the beauty and magic unfold because of its power. I have personally experienced the bountiful, blissful, and beautiful transformations that take place because of it, and have witnessed the magic it performs in many other women's lives as well.

Yogi Bhajan and his teachings are the link to the miracle you and I have been searching for to feel 'good enough'. His precious and timely insights regarding our *energy being* uncover the secrets inside our physiology that bring forth our true greatness. As a sacred being, his teachings radiate light into the darkness and help us see more clearly our highest selves! I have been astounded by the profound effects this scientific technology has had in my own life and felt guided to share it with you. It is with great sadness that I relate to you that Yogi Bhajan transitioned from his physical life on October 6th, 2004. However, I know his spirit is still alive through his teachings as I have come to know him through them and felt his spirit with me while writing this book, and this very special chapter.

Yogi Bhajan is the fifth and final *Enlightened Master of Our Time* I share with you in this book. I am grateful for the privilege to expose these teachings to you with permission from the Kundalini Research Institute [KRI]. You can learn more about Yogi Bhajan and the KRI at www.kundaliniresearchinstitute.com. I am most grateful to Yogi Bhajan for the profound moments of beauty, power, healing, magic, and miracles I have experienced because of his teachings.

What is Kundalini Yoga?

Kundalini Yoga builds the strength in you. You become you. Then all of your fears and all of your conflicts and all of your duality goes away, your reality starts coming because you are very attractive. The attraction is not you. It is your radiant body—the shining armor around you for protection and attraction. And it all depends on how deeply you consume prana, and how often every day you breathe absolutely mechanically, not automatically.
—Yogi Bhajan, December 17, 1997.

The Secret Power of Kundalini Yoga

The power of Kundalini Yoga lies in the actual experience. It goes right into your heart and extends your consciousness so you may have a wider horizon of grace and of knowing the truth. Ultimately you come to understand your existence in relationship to the universe and understand that you already are, and this brings you to the practical experience of infinity. You can then radiate creativity and infinity in all aspects of your daily life.
—Yogi Bhajan

Kundalini Yoga as taught by Yogi Bhajan® is not a religion, but rather an ancient, sacred science and technology. Often referred to as the *Yoga of Awareness,* it awakens the flow of *Kundalini* or a latent force that moves through each of our eight *chakras* or *energy centres* in the body (*sacral, root, navel, heart, throat, third eye, crown, aura*) to influence the right balance to optimize our living and being in the mind, body, and spirit. A perfect technology for our Western society because of its fast and efficient results, Kundalini Yoga holds the secret to living and being at the highest vibrations where we meet up with the power of the divine field of energy in the universe to support our lives. To live in harmony with this higher level of energy, the mind, body, and spirit are challenged as they transform on a cellular level to become one with this intelligent source of power. Kundalini Yoga as taught by Yogi Bhajan® masterfully raises our vibrational level of energy and our level of consciousness, simultaneously.

One truly has to practice this yoga to know the magical effects it delivers as it directly balances and influences the glandular system, the nervous system, and the mind, while it shares a direct link to the path that unveils the truth about who you really are. It guides us to overcome the challenges of the mind, body, and spirit. Because we are all unique, everyone's experience with the energy within them during this practice is also unique. It is important to remember that not everyone will experience physical sensations as kundalini awakens inside the body, but some will. When my own kundalini energy began to rise up through my chakras I could feel a comforting warm and tingly sensation in my lungs. As I related earlier in the book, I just happened to be recovering from pneumonia at the time. It was a humbling experience to know the power of this technology face to face, as it carefully and consciously seemed to know where to exert its healing power inside my body. I remember thinking, "how beautiful and intelligent this kundalini force is." My body continues to communicate ongoing secrets, messages, and warm tingling sensations as the brilliant wisdom and knowledge of this sacred science communicates its gentle, yet powerful presence to me. I am drawn to the comfort, protection, and divine guidance it offers through dedicated practice, or as we have come to know it in this book, *sacred sadhana*. Take note of the unique messages your mind, body, and spirit send you. Kundalini Yoga has empowered me to know that we are all much greater beings with more creative power than we have ever been taught or led to believe through mainstream social learning and the mass media.

Let's not forget that Kundalini Yoga was secretly practiced by elite members of society. Although hidden over the ages, it is now courageously revealed to us by Yogi Bhajan. We are blessed to experience the powerful gifts this intelligent science shares with us. I relate often throughout this book that we are *energy beings* and there is no other more powerful *energy system balancer* and *optimizer* than Kundalini Yoga as taught by Yogi Bhajan®. It is an intense workout for the mind, body, and spirit that shares pure magic and miracles as it heals, balances, divinely enlightens, reaches every intention, and unveils the REAL you! I promise that you will love it!

Kundalini Yoga balances the glandular system, strengthens the 72,000 nerves in the body, expands the lung capacity, and purifies the blood stream. It brings balance to the body, mind, and soul. It teaches positive, self-empowering attitudes of thinking. It is on the job training for success and excellence in life. It builds inner strength and self-awareness so you can fulfill your highest potential.
—Shakti Parwa Kaur Khalsa

Magical Gifts

We have already learned that bringing honor and reverence to any other insights and practices we choose to apply from this book intensifies our results and magnifies our vibration—it is the secret of all secrets shared in the *Sacred Sadhana* chapter. Similar to this deep secret, Kundalini Yoga as taught by Yogi Bhajan® causes extraordinarily powerful results because of the impressive combination of scientific technologies in one scientific practice (*postures, mudras, sacred mantras, meditations, breath practice, bandhas, and eye focus*). Take hold of the beautiful secrets and gifts Kundalini Yoga shares. Some of the blessings I have received from my own practice include; a sense of peace and contentment, physical and emotional healing, self-love (*I celebrate and honor who I am*), clarity (*sage-like knowing*), inspiration (*masterfully guided to purpose*), higher consciousness (*connected to divine wisdom*), abundance, prosperity, synchronistic events, protection from harm, the release of fear and addictions, and an overall sense of feeling empowered and self-actualized. As I have already related, I have experienced countless synchronistic miracles while studying and practicing this technology, and while writing this book.

Special Guidelines

Because of the powerful and sacred nature of this technology, it is advised to practice Kundalini Yoga as taught by Yogi Bhajan® separate from any other healing exercises or practices. Consult a physician as one would do before adding any physical activity to your daily practice. The benefits attributed to the practice of Kundalini Yoga stem from centuries-old yogic traditions and results will vary for every individual. Kundalini Yoga should not be practiced while under the influence of alcohol or drugs.

The Secrets in Sadhana

The greatest reward of doing sadhana is that the person becomes incapable of being defeated. Sadhana is a self-victory, and it is a victory over time and space. Getting up in the morning is a victory over time, and doing it is a victory over space.
—Yogi Bhajan

We have already learned that *Sadhana* is a daily sacred practice we become dedicated to, to bring forth our greatness! When our commitment to it is consistent and saturated with heartfelt honor and reverence, we make it sacred—and magic happens!

Sparkling Insight

To increase the flow of the sun's energy into the body from the crown or seventh chakra (the energy centre at the top of the head), keep your hair contained under and covered with a natural piece of cloth. The science behind the covering of the head allows this flow of energy to pass unimpeded downward so it can activate the upward rising of kundalini energy from the radiant solar plexus.

My Sacred Space

The following information is a description of the sacred space I prepare for myself to blend high energy vibrations into my practice area along with the power of my Kundalini Yoga practice.

I find a peaceful atmosphere and ensure that I come to practice with a mindset bathed in honor, reverence, and an intention dear to my heart in the moment. I have a warm throw blanket, a pillow, soothing vibrational music, and a yoga mat ready for use. I burn some healing incense, diffuse essential oils, smudge native medicinal herbs, and surround this space with high energy gemstones and some candlelight. My spirit name (*Akal Sahai Kaur:* meaning *undying and connected to the infinite power*) written on a special card and a photo of Yogi Bhajan are placed on the table in this space as well. Allow your own intuition to guide you to what should be present to make your own practice sacred for you.

Glossary of Terms

I have inserted some definitions below to help you understand the Kundalini Yoga meditations I share with you in this chapter.

Breath/Pranayama: I have discussed breath in detail in chapter 17. You are already aware of the power of our breath as it creates life itself. When we spend time practicing breath *[pranayama]* we create optimum function of the cells in our bodies and thus manifest our ability to optimize our living and being in magical ways we have never known. Pranayama is an ancient and sacred scientific practice used in yoga.

Posture/Asana: The position we hold our bodies in to improve the health and function of the body. The science of yoga involves creating angles and triangles with the body so life force can flow through it. As specific muscles and pressure points are activated through asana, the body function optimizes as it works to communicate body wisdom, clear energy blocks, improve the flow of energy to an intended area, and bring balance to all of the energy systems inside the body over time.

Sparkling Insight

Look at the power behind some secret angles the body can create.

While lying down on your back, lift legs

- *0-12 inches to connect to creativity and influence the following organs: sex organs (ovaries, uterus), digestive glands, intestines, and eliminating glands*

  In general this degree of angle affects everything below the navel point

- *0-6 inches to influence ovaries/sex glands*

- *6-18 inches to influence the navel point and kidneys*

- *12 inches-2 feet to influence the liver, spleen, gall bladder, and pancreas*

- *1½ feet-2½ feet to influence the liver, upper stomach, and gall bladder*

- *2-3 feet to influence the heart, lungs, and stomach*

- *over 4 feet-90 degrees to influence the thyroid, parathyroid, and pineal gland*

- *90 degrees (shoulder stand) to influence the pineal and pituitary glands, and memory*

Note: Lifting the arms upward to a 60 degree angle can positively influence both the heart and lungs.

Mantra: a combination of words more powerful than a simple affirmation. The words in a mantra are sacred and scientifically chosen to create a vibration inside the body when repeated. These words also tap out a pattern on the eighty-four reflex points on the roof of the mouth that set off a multitude of physiological changes to help regulate all of the systems of the body. A myriad of positive effects can happen including: a connection to divine consciousness, renewed brain patterns, altered mood states, and balance throughout the entire neuroendocrine system. All of these effects transport us to beautiful and optimal states of living and being. Each vibratory wave of a mantra settles in the body cells and draws to it matching vibrations.

Sparkling Insight

Yogi Bhajan often taught meditations chanting mantras acapella: without music. This experience requires stillness so only the sound current created with your own voice is heard and felt within. The physical body is played like an instrument. If music is included in a meditation it must contain a specific rhythm as guided by Yogi Bhajan.

Eye Focus: Many Kundalini Yoga meditations include a specific position for the eyes. These positions create an effect on the optic nerve to cause direct changes on the glandular systems and the brain itself. If no eye position is specified you can close the eyes and focus at the brow point (center of the forehead).

Mudras: As we have related earlier in the book, the hands contain specific energy points that positively affect different body regions when pressed, massaged, stretched, or specifically positioned, similar to the body map that exists in foot reflexology. This is not unlike the body map imprinted on the sensory-motor cortex of the brain. Like a treasure map, there are some secret jewels to be found when these body maps are understood and utilized. The energy and consciousness within the hands communicates with the mind, body, and spirit mystically, and reminds us we are energy beings.

The hands are an energy map of our consciousness and health.
—Yogi Bhajan

The magic our fingers hold is related in the following chart.

SIGN	FINGER	MUDRA NAME	EFFECT
(The tip of each finger indicated below connects with a thumb tip to create a mudra and the effect listed)			
Jupiter	Index	Gyan Mudra	Knowledge
Saturn	Middle	Shuni Mudra	Wisdom, Intelligence, Patience
Sun	Ring	Surya Mudra	Vitality, Energy
Mercury	Pinkie	Buddhi Mudra	Ability to communicate

Prayer Pose: Bring the palms of both hands together. Your fingers should be pointing upward and pressed together while thumbs press against the sternum at the center of the chest. This hand position neutralizes the positive side of the body (right, sun, masculine) with the negative side (left, moon, feminine).

Sparkling Insight

THE SECRET POWER BEHIND PRAYER POSE

There is a science to using Pranam Mudra. There is a polarity in the body between the right side, the pingala, and left side, the ida. When you put the right and left hands together, you are neutralizing the positive and negative polarities of the electromagnetic field. This action creates a neutral space in the electromagnetic field. The position of the knuckles of the thumbs – in the notch of the breastbone – is a reflex point for the vagus nerve, one of the major nerves going to the pineal gland up the front of the body. This pressure immediately causes the pineal and pituitary glands to secrete, creating a resonance in the brain that moves it out of its normal rhythm to a meditative state. This allows one's prayer to come from the heart.—3HO

Body Locks (Bandhas): specific alignments we choose for the body during the practice of Kundalini Yoga as taught by Yogi Bhajan®. When performed, they direct the flow of incoming and outgoing prana (life force) and apana (eliminating force) which in turn softly combine and awaken the kundalini energy that sits at the base of the spine.

A SECRET GIFT
Part One

Look to the center of your own Bountiful, Blissful, Beautiful Healing Mantra Card or the one available on the *shop* area of my website @ www.realbeautiful.ca.

I have given no explanation for the sacred mantra *Sat Nam* that I secretly placed on the center of this healing mantra card to help heal and empower women of all ages. The card is already imprinted with the mystical energy and power of Yogi Bhajan's own sacred words for women (I am bountiful, blissful, beautiful, bountiful, blissful, beautiful, I am). I knew adding *Sat Nam* as a second mantra would greatly increase the magical power of this card. Uncover the secret power behind this mantra as you find out more about it below and throughout this chapter.

Sat Nam: referred to as the *Bij Mantra*. It is the most frequently used mantra in the practice of Kundalini Yoga.

Sat: means truth.

Nam: means identity.

As you repetitively chant the words *Sat Nam* (pronounced Sut Numb) listen to your inner voice as it guides you to deeper self-knowledge. You will know who you are, why you are here, and the gifts and talents you have been given to share with the world! This mantra magically and mystically guides you to the truth of your being.

Listen to the pronunciation of *Sat Nam* at kundalini research institute. org/tools4teachers/toolsforteachers_3.htm

A SECRET GIFT
Part Two (A)

Uncover even more beautiful secrets behind the power of the mantra *Sat Nam* when it is separated into the five primal sounds contained within it, also known as, the *panj shabd*: sa, ta, na, ma, aa. These powerful sounds share even more secrets that you will find out about in the *Addictions Meditation* further on in this chapter.

Let's Begin…

Kundalini Yoga as taught by Yogi Bhajan® should always begin with 'tuning in' and end with *The Long Time Sun* prayer. These two elements help to ensure safe and effective practice.

Tune In

Tune In/Prayer Pose

Body Posture/Asana: Sit in *easy pose* (cross-legged) as shown in the illustration.

Body Lock/Jalandhar Bandh (Neck Lock): the spine and neck should be straight while keeping the muscles of the neck and throat firm by lifting the chest upward and at the same time gently stretching the back of the neck upwards with the head staying level and centered. Do not tilt the head forward.

Mudra/Hand Position: Hold your hands in prayer pose (holding the palms and fingers of your hands together while all fingers and thumbs are pointing upward) while the thumbs press against the center of the breastbone/sternum.

Breath/Pranayama: Breathe in deeply through the nose and the breath will naturally be released as you chant the 'adi mantra' below.

Mantra/Healing Sound Vibration: (Adi Mantra) Ong Namo Guru Dev Namo *(I bow to the subtle infinite wisdom, the divine teacher within).*

Eye Position: Closed

Repeat this sequence 3-5 times

Health Benefits:

- Chanting this mantra connects you to the 'golden chain' of teachers of Kundalini Yoga. It prepares you to gracefully receive all of the other benefits of the Kundalini Yoga set that follows.

* *My Preference: I personally like to add an intention to guide my practice as I tune in. What do you want to release or bring to you? Listen to the voice inside as it guides you to the right intention.*

* *Listen to the pronunciation of the Adi Mantra (Ong Namo Guru Dev Namo) at* kundaliniresearchinstitute.org/tools4teachers/toolsforteachers_3.htm

This ends the "tuning in" process.

WARM-UP

If you wish you may choose to do one or more of the following exercises below to prepare you for the meditations shared in this chapter. Always breathe in and out through your nose unless guided to do otherwise. As a health professional, I feel it is important to warm the body up before any exercise.

> *If you want things to be done for you so you don't have to do anything, then you must breathe from one to five or six breaths per minute. If you can practice that then you can attract the universe to you.*
> —Yogi Bhajan

Sitali Pranayam

Body Posture/Asana: Sit in easy pose.

Body Lock/Jalandhar Bandh (Light Neck Lock): the spine and neck should be straight while keeping the muscles of the neck and throat firm by lifting the chest upward and at the same time gently stretching the back of the neck upward with the head staying level and centered. Do not tilt the head forward.

* Roll the tongue into a 'U' with the tip protruding just beyond the lips.

Breath/Pranayama: breathe in deeply through your rolled 'U' tongue and breathe out through your nose.

Eye Position: You may choose to close your eyes and focus on the center of the forehead (brow point).

Breath Pattern: repeat the sequence above for three minutes, or 26 times morning and evening. When repeated 108 times, this breath practice becomes a powerful healer for the body and the digestive system.

Health Benefits:

- power, strength, and vitality
- has a cooling and cleansing effect on the mind, body, and spirit
- detoxification of the body *(a bitter taste on your tongue indicates a cleansing effect and will disappear in time, while a sweet taste indicates a sign of balanced health)*

> *People who practice this kriya have all things come to them that they need by the planet ether. In mystical terms, you are served by the heavens.*
> —Yogi Bhajan

Spinal Twist

Spinal Twist Pose

Body Posture/Asana: Sit in *easy pose*. Bring your right hand up to grab your right shoulder and your left hand to grab your left with the thumbs in back and fingers in front as shown. Next, twist your upper body from the waist to your left as you breathe in through your nose and to your right as you breathe out through your nose.

Body Lock/Jalandhar Bandh (Neck Lock): the spine and neck should be straight while keeping the muscles of the neck and throat firm by lifting the chest upward and at the same time gently stretching the back of the neck upwards with the head staying level and centered. Do not tilt the head forward.

Mudra/Hand Position: Hands are holding right and left shoulders respectively while the four fingers are in front of the shoulders and thumbs are behind.

Breath/Pranayama: Breathe in through the nose as you twist to the left with hands on your shoulders. Breathe out through your nose as you twist to the right.

Mantra/Healing Sound Vibration: Silently repeat *Sat* as you inhale and twist upper body to the left and *Nam* as you exhale and twist to the right.

Eye Position: close your eyes and focus on your third eye (center of your forehead).

*Repeat this sequence for up to three minutes. Do not reverse the breath.

Listen to the pronunciation of the mantra Sat Nam at kundalinir esearchinstitute.org/tools4teachers/toolsforteachers_3.htm

Heath Benefits:
- flexibility and circulation to the spine
- encourages the movement of kundalini energy up through the chakras

Miracle Bend

Miracle Bend Pose

This posture is a sequence that flows from one position to another mixed with breath practice. Follow the flow of instructions below to complete. Eyes can be closed.

1. As you stand tall with shoulders back, bring your legs, knees, and heels together so they touch.

2. Your feet should be placed flat on the ground with right and left big toes pointing outward for balance.

3. Raise both of your arms in unison above your head resting them close to your ears and along the side of your head with your palms facing away from you.

4. While keeping the legs straight begin to bend backwards from the lower part (base) of your spine approximately twenty degrees. It is natural for your body to shake. Let your upper body form an *arc* beginning at the base of the spine upwards to the tip of the head. Continue to keep legs straight as guided above.

5. Hold this posture for two minutes as you breathe long, deep, and gentle breath cycles (one complete breath cycle is one long deep inhalation followed by one long and deep exhalation).

6. After two minutes, to end, take in a breath and gently come to a standing posture. Continue to keep you palms and arms together and close to the ears and head.

7. Release the breath and the posture. Relax.

Health Benefits:
- calms the nervous system
- diffuses anger and calms unbalanced emotions
- brings healing and balance to the female reproductive organs
- releases insecurity

Sparkling Insight

Our 'beauty glands', also known as the thyroid and parathyroid glands, when activated through Kundalini Yoga, uplift our mood, increase metabolism, increase energy, support growth of bones and teeth, and stimulate the function of the adrenal glands, the nervous system, and the gonads (sex organs).

Kundalini Yoga Meditations

Siri Gaitri Mantra Meditation for Healing (ra ma da sa sa say so hung)

Siri Gaitri Meditation Pose

Body Posture/Asana: Sit in easy pose.

Body Lock/Jalandhar Bandh (Light Neck Lock): the spine and neck should be straight while keeping the muscles of the neck and throat firm by lifting the chest upward and at the same time gently stretching the back of the neck upwards with the head staying level and centered. Do not tilt the head forward.

Mudra/Hand Position:

1. Tuck your elbows in snug to the sides of your body and ribs.

2. Bend the hands to create flattened palms facing upward as the tips of the fingers point further outward away from the sides of the body.

3. The palms of the hands should stay flat and facing upward while bent at the wrists. Keep fingers side by side and you should feel a slight pull in the wrists at the bend.

4. Do your best to keep the palms flat throughout the kriya. (see illustration)

Breath/Pranayama: Take a long deep breath in through your nose and as you slowly release it chant *ra ma da sa sa say so hung* on the breath you exhale. As you say *hung* at the end of your breath pull the navel point (belly button area) in towards your spine sharply.

Mantra/Healing Sound Vibration: This mantra is called the *Siri Gaitri Mantra* which contains the eight basic sounds (ra ma da sa sa say so hung) carried within the sacred naad (sound of the universe) which captures the healing light of the cosmos.

Eye Position: eyes are closed.

Repeat this sequence for 11-31 minutes.

Listen to the pronunciation of the ra, ma, da, sa, sa, say, so hung mantra at kundaliniresearchinstitute.org/tools4teachers/toolsforteachers_3.htm (Siri Gaitri Mantra)

Sparkling Insight:

This mantra is one of the most powerful and beautiful ones given to us by Yogi Bhajan. Learn more about the power it holds below.

Ra: uses the sun's vibration to boost energy and purity

Ma: uses the energy of the moon to improve receptivity, and to cool and nurture us

Da: uses earth's energy to bring security and a sense of being grounded

Sa: brings forth infinity on all levels of expansiveness

Say: embodies the sacred or essence of Saa

So: means identity, I

Hung: the infinite, thou, (*So Hung* together means *I am Thou*)

To end this beautiful meditation:

1. Inhale deeply and retain this breath inside you as you visualize the individual(s) you wish to heal, even if this vision includes you. See this person completely engulfed in white light fully healed and vibrant.

2. Exhale and inhale deeply one more time, retain this breath inside you as you send this healing prayer to the universe.

3. Lift your arms up high and shake them along with your hands and fingers. Relax.

Health Benefits:

- this mantra is considered a jewel among all the sacred Kundalini Yoga knowledge handed down to us by Yogi Bhajan. I have experienced profound healing and infinity as the vibration of these words echoed inside my mind, body, and spirit.

- brings forth powerful healing on multiple levels because of the eight sacred sounds chanted within the mantra.

- because it contains the eight sacred sounds that stimulate the flow of kundalini through one of the major channels (nadis) in the body up the centre of the spine, it is also considered *Sushmana Mantra* and thus heightens and widens the effects this one mantra can have. Each sound plays a role in resonating different transformations.

- unites us to infinity and purity.

- balances the right and left hemispheres of the brain to create a neutral mind which brings forth intuition and awareness that reveals one's purpose and destiny.

- creates metabolic balance.

Meditation for Addictions and Breaking Unhealthy Patterns

Healing Addictions Meditation Pose

Body Posture/Asana: Sit in easy pose.

Body Lock/Jalandhar Bandh (Light Neck Lock): the spine and neck should be straight while keeping the muscles of the neck and throat firm by lifting the chest upward and at the same time gently stretching the back of the neck upwards with the head staying level and centered. Do not tilt the head forward.

Mudra/Hand Position: Make a fist with both hands but extend the thumbs straight. Place the pad of each thumb on the respective temple. Find the notch or indent at the temples and rest the thumbs in it.

Breath/Pranayama: No breath specified.

Mantra/Healing Sound Vibration: Lock the back molars together and keep the lips closed. Alternately squeeze the molars tightly and then release the pressure on them to the rhythm of the mantra *sa ta na ma aa* (also known as the five primal sounds called *the panj shabd*). A muscle will move in rhythm under the thumbs. Silently vibrate the five primal sounds *sa ta na ma* aa while you squeeze and release pressure on the molars. Feel this action massage the thumbs while maintaining a firm pressure with the hands. (See illustration).

Eye Position: close your eyes and focus on your third eye (center of your forehead).

A SECRET GIFT
Part Two (B)

The second gift in the mantra *Sat Nam* is revealed when we break the mantra down and the magic power of the Panj Shabd (sa ta na ma aa) is exposed. Read below the find out more about the gifts this secret mantra shares when it is separated into pieces!

Remember, when you recite the panj shabd you will recite these sounds silently in your mind. The information below gives you an understanding of the gifts these primal sounds share when silently recited repetitively.

Sa: is the sound of infinity, the cosmos and the beginning

Ta: is the sound of life, existence

Na: is the sound of conquering death, change or transformation

Ma: is the sound of rebirth, new life

Aa: is the sound of coming forth

Listen to these five primal sounds or panj shabd mantra at kundalini researchinstitute.org/tools4teachers/toolsforteachers_3.htm

* This meditation has a tremendous effect on the pituitary gland which is required to heal addictions. It sends a rhythmic current into the central brain and re-sets the balance in the pineal gland which in turn balances the glandular system in the body.

Sparkling Insight

The pineal and pituitary glands are called 'divine glands' because they have the power to connect us to higher consciousness and balance our glandular organs. When these glands are activated while practicing the 'addictions meditation', the patterns that keep addictions alive, disappear.

* Continue the meditation above for 3-7 minutes and increase to 20-31 minutes over time. This beautiful meditation brings healing and radiance to the divine glands.

To End: At the end of this set, place your hands in *Gyan Mudra* on your knees in easy pose and breath in and out through the nose for 3 minutes.

Health Benefits:

- We live in a very challenging time. Stress and anxiety are at an all-time high, desperately driving us to find ways to stabilize our mind, body, and spirit. When we understand that we are energy beings we can activate the healing doctor within us to soothe and comfort us. We learn to change our automatic reflexes that drive us towards destructive ways of living and being and we can reset the messages and patterns within us. Knowing the ways to soothe our own chemistry within is required. I offer this very timely meditation to heal the disrupted patterns we all contain within. Be honest with yourself and identify the patterns you know you would like to release and slowly incorporate this meditation into a *sacred sadhana* for 40 days, all by itself. The power behind it will astound you. This meditation is one of the gifts left to us by Yogi Bhajan to help us survive the Aquarian Age. Addictions take hold under the stem of the pineal gland where the imbalances make it impossible for habits to be broken. The rhythm that balances the pineal gland is disturbed and needs to be reset. This meditation will do it. This meditation covers all addictions, both mental and physical such as: substance abuse, patterns of disordered eating, irrational fears, the need to feel accepted by others, cravings for emotional love, shoe addictions, and so many more.

The Last Resort Meditation [for Depression]

June 15, 1982

The Last Resort Meditation Pose

Body Posture/Asana: Sit in 'easy pose' with a straight spine with your hands in your lap, palms up. Your right hand rests in left hand while your thumb tips touch.

Mudra/Hand Position: Place your hands in your lap with your palms facing up and let thumb tips touch.

Breath/Pranayama: Breathe in as slowly and as deeply as you can. Then, let your breath go slowly while you chant the mantra, eight times.

Mantra/Healing Sound Vibration: Wahe Guru, Wahe Guru, Wahe Guru, Wahe Jeo (Ecstasy Mantra).

* *The spelling of Gurbani words are often changed to support the pronunciation of the words in the mantra..*

WHAA-HAY GUROO, WHAA-HAY GUROO, WHAA-HAY GUROO, WHAA-HAY JEE-O

Eye Position: eyes are closed.

Repeat this breath sequence and mantra for eleven minutes maximum to start. Gradually increase to 22 minutes, then 33 minutes.

Listen to the pronunciation of the *Ecstasy Mantra* at spiritvoyage.com when you listen to a sample of it on Seda Begcan's "Sunrise" album.

A sample of the first part of this mantra can also be heard at the link below. Although it does not contain the word *jee-o* in it, it is still helpful to hear the rhythm and most of the sounds within the mantra. *kundaliniresearchinstitute.org/tools4teachers/toolsforteachers_3.htm.*

Health Benefits:
- creates relaxation
- builds strength
- creates mental clarity
- connects us to infinity (divine source)
- decreases depression and negativity
- elevates bliss/happiness

Three Minute Har [Prosperity Meditation]

I believe it is our birthright to be prosperous. This meditation aligns you with the vibrations that draw prosperity towards you. Watch the magic happen as you observe riches enter your life!

The Three Minute Har Meditation Pose

Close-up Palms Up

*Close-up Palms Down
with Thumbs Crossed*

Body Posture/Asana: Sit in easy pose.

Body Lock/Jalandhar Bandh (Light Neck Lock): the spine and neck should be straight while keeping the muscles of the neck and throat firm by lifting the chest upward and at the same time gently stretching the back of the neck upwards with the head staying level and centered. Do not tilt the head forward.

Mudra/Hand Position: place your arms at your sides and bend them at the elbows as your forearms, hands, and fingers diagonally extend upwards in front of you at the level of the throat. Hit the side of your hands so that the sides of the pinkie fingers meet as palms face upward. Flip the hands over so palms are down as the sides of index fingers hit/touch while your right thumb slides underneath the left thumb. Alternately hit each side of the hands as related above in a rhythm with the mantra *har*. Repeat the word *har* as you hit the sides of your upward palms and pinkies, and then chant it again as you turn your palms down and hit the sides of your index fingers with thumbs crossed, right under left. With each *har*, pull the navel centre (*in the area of your belly button*) sharply inwards towards the spine.

Breath/Pranayama: find your own breath rhythm.

Mantra/Healing Sound Vibration: Har.

On each repetition the navel is pulled in and the tip of the tongue flicks off the roof of the mouth.

Eye Position: look at the tip of your nose with your eyes 1/10th open.

Yogi Bhajan tells us that there is no need to exceed eleven minutes for this practice to ensure we do not become greedy.

Listen to the pronunciation of the *har* mantra at spiritvoyage.com in a sample of Gurudass Kaur's album titled *Kundalini Mantra Instruction*.

Miracle Mantra Meditation

A final gift....

When this mantra is recited with intention, honor, and reverence; prayers are answered.

* Focus on an intention as you recite this Gurbani miracle mantra 11 times.

Ardas Bhaee

Amar Das Guroo

Amar Das Guru, Ardhas Bhaee

Raam Daas Guroo, Raam Daas Guroo

Raam Daas Guroo, Sachee Sahee

Mantra Translation: The prayer has been given to Guru Amar Das. The prayer is manifested by Guru Ram Das (*The Lord of Miracles*). The miracle is complete.

Listen to a pronunciation of this mantra at spiritvoyage.com from a sample of Snatam Kaur's *Liberation's Door* album.

Closing Prayer

Every Kundalini Yoga set should end with the prayer that follows. Cover yourself with a soft and warm blanket in savasana *(lay on your back with your arms and legs spread at about 45 degrees and close your eyes)* while you recite this closing prayer allow your mind, body, and spirit to rest.

The Long Time Sun

May the long time sun shine upon you.

All love surround you,

And the light within you,

Guide your way on.

Sat Nam

A Beautiful Way to Experience and Learn Kundalini Yoga Mantras

In my study of Kundalini Yoga as taught by Yogi Bhajan® I found it helpful to listen to the mantras included in the meditations by one of my favorite artists, Snatam Kaur. You can listen to samples of her music through Spirit Voyage (spiritvoyage.com) or The Source (thesource.kriteachings.org). I was mystically drawn to Snatum Kaur's voice while writing this book. It is her voice that led me to the sacred teachings of Yogi Bhajan. I intended to meet Snatam Kaur similar to how I met Dr. Wayne Dyer and I was blessed to meet her at a concert held in London, Ontario. Our meeting stands as a wonderful memory to cherish and one more demonstration of how magic and miracles can take place in life when we align ourselves with the vibration of the divine source and intend them to show up through *sacred sadhana*. Sat Nam.

The purpose of life is to be beautiful, to be bountiful, to be blissful, to be graceful and grateful.
—Yogi Bhajan

Chapter 20

BONUS GIFT:
Shining Expert Insights

Your task is not to seek for love, but merely to seek and find
all the barriers within yourself that you have built against it.
—*Rumi*

The Greatest Gift

*W*HEN OUR MINDS ARE OPEN to receive the greatness of others to support our living and being, we become synergistically empowered. Like being showered with gifts on our birthday, we receive the polished diamonds they are giving away if we are willing to listen. I believe that every individual has his or her own genius, an area of concentration of knowledge that is unique and rare like a diamond, because that individual has spent a lifetime acquiring it.

There are not enough hours in the day for each of us to spend the hours that someone else has studying to refine certain knowledge. I am honored to have come to know the greatness of each of the following experts. They all have touched my life in some way, causing it to sparkle brighter because of the light they shine in the world. It is with deep gratitude, honor, and reverence that I thank each of them for the opportunity to include their insights in this book. The vibrational energy of this book is higher because of them.

Cultivating Radiance Tips by Tamara Gerlach

We are blessed to glance at the energy-expanding and radiant insights of Tamara Gerlach, the best-selling author of Cultivating Radiance: Five Essential Elements for Holistic Self Care. In my experience in knowing Tamara, she emits a radiant light wherever she goes. Her loving heart and undeniable spirit echo in behind her talent as an author, a business and life coach, a mentor, a radio show host, and a former National Team coach. Tam lives and breathes the meaning of REAL Beautiful as her life exudes pure love, beauty, and the essence of magic and miracles. Connect with Tamara through her website at TamaraGerlach.com.

How to Cultivate Radiance

Radiance is our inner light that reflects on our outside. It's the joy and passion that comes through all that we do. Sometimes we get so busy taking care of everyone and everything else that our light starts to dim. The good news is that self-care is the foundation of radiance, and we can get it back at any time by simply caring for ourselves. It may seem like a foreign concept at times, but it's totally doable.

The benefits of cultivating your radiance begin with developing healthy relationships, especially the one with yourself. When we are taking fabulous care of ourselves, everything around us begins to align and get into harmony. By looking into our beliefs and attitudes, we can awaken our passion and create a vision for the life that we want.

1. Know Your Faucets and Drains

What do we live for, if it is not to make life
less difficult for each other?
—George Eliot

Some people and things in our lives are faucets. Others are drains. Faucets are the people and things that inspire us, give us energy, and make us feel alive. They can be anything: from a relationship that stretches and grows us to activities like walking in nature, playing guitar, or lovemaking. Drains, on the other hand, are those people and things that lower our vibration, bring us down, and make us feel stuck. These can include relationships with toxic people; perhaps those who have bomber attitudes, like to gossip, or are constantly taking from us without giving anything in return. Drains could also be activities, such as unfulfilling work or not taking care of your body and mind.

Take a moment to write down five things and five people who are faucets in your life. Once you have that list of five people and five things, next to each item describe how it acts as a faucet in your life. Why does it make you feel so good? Then, do the same for your drains, considering why each is so draining.

Now, spend as much time as possible with your faucets and cut out or spend as little time as possible with your drains.

2. Use Your Radiance Superpowers

These are the strengths we possess that come easily and naturally, and in most cases, we take them for granted. You may think, "Well, anyone can do that." Actually, no, they can't. Nobody has your gifts, talents, skills, tools, and experiences … and no one has alchemized them in the same unique way that creates your special offering to the world.

What I love about our RSPs is that we never criticize ourselves for having them. Passion is one of my superpowers, and I never say to myself, "Man, I wish I were less passionate." Creativity is another; again, I never wish I were less creative. Write down an exhaustive list of all of the things that you are awesome at, and highlight your top three. These three are your "super strengths" that are always there for you. When life gets tough, you can always fall back on them. So rather than shrinking back when we face resistance or challenges, we can slip into our proverbial phone booth and come out with our super powers to save the day!

3. Ground Your Energy

Energy is such an amazing tool when we use it to our advantage. Physically, it gives us strength, keeps us from being dragged around by our emotions, and connects us to the Divine. Becoming aware of what helps you get grounded will help you become unshakable.

What does it take for you to become physically grounded, in balance, and strong? It feels like trying to pick up a child who doesn't want to be picked up, where we press our weight into the earth and feel solid. Practice grounding your body and notice how solid it feels.

Pay attention to how it feels when you are emotionally grounded (or not). What is it like in your body? What are the thoughts that go through your mind?

Another aspect of grounding is our connection to the Divine or spiritual connection. So with our feet on the ground and our emotions in the body, the spirit has the freedom to connect with All That Is: the beauty, grace, and flow of the Divine.

I'd like to invite you to have a couple of mantras available for when you feel yourself slipping, to remind yourself to be physically, emotionally, and spiritually grounded, and to bring back your radiance.

4. Be Outrageously Optimistic

> *Silent gratitude isn't much use to anyone.*
> —Gladys Berthe Stern

Can you imagine going through life being happy, appreciative, and positive almost all of the time? It's easy to get caught up in what's wrong with the world, but the truth is that we are 100 percent responsible for our own feelings. No one and nothing can *make* us feel anything. Our attitude doesn't have to be dragged around by the news, the economy, nor what is going on around us; we can actually choose how we look at life.

Practicing living with an outrageously positive attitude doesn't mean shutting our eyes, covering our ears, and pretending that everything is "perfect." It does mean creating a solid foundation of positive feelings about who we are and how we operate in the world, so that when times do get tough, rather than allowing them to take us down, we can meet our challenges with confidence that we will get through it and we will be okay.

Be outrageously optimistic by looking for what's good in our life. When you wake up every morning, immediately think of at least five awesome things about your life, even before you get out of bed. These can be as simple as "I'm still alive!" or appreciating the people and luxuries you have in your life.

5. Ignite Your Passionate Dream

Never give up on the things you love in order to do
the things that don't matter.
—Cultivating Radiance

Paying attention to our passion wakes up every cell in the body; we tingle, our heart races, and we feel completely alive. Being passionate about life is living life to its fullest, to the edge, doing the absolute best we can. We put our heart into everything we do and dream big!

A radiant life begins with a passionate dream. Our dreams give us direction and are ever expanding. We open our hearts and our minds to the possibility that we could do, be, and have all that our heart desires. When our passion is ignited, we are filled with enthusiasm and optimism. Embrace life with a full heart, spark your creativity, inspire, give your life meaning, rediscover what you love, or discover new passions.

Take a moment to write down your passionate dream of a radiant life and then share it. Get the support you need to bring your dream to life.

6. Bust the Status Quo

First they ignore you, then they laugh at you,
then they fight you, then you win.
—*Gandhi*

Is there any part of your life that you just do because that is the way it's always been done or because you fear that if you change people might not like it? Let go of those thoughts and explore what else is possible. Radiant people are *bold*, daring, and innovative. Life is far too short to stay in the box of mediocrity, doing and thinking the same ol' standard stuff. The status quo will suffocate your radiance.

It takes *courage* to be free from our limiting thoughts. Being fearless doesn't mean that we have *no* fear; it means that we don't let our fear control our lives or undermine our dreams. Wake up your light, shake up the situation, risk being uncomfortable, and take the chance to come alive!

Ask yourself: "What would be the boldest move to make right now?" Then do that!

7. Explore Your Divine Feminine

Take a few minutes every day to explore your own beauty. How is it showing up today? Are you feeling loving and nurturing or, like Mother Nature, sometimes needing to destroy and create something new? Maybe you are feeling like a muse, playful and sassy, or, like Aphrodite, drawing love and sensuality toward you. The beauty of being a woman is that we are all of these and so much more. And we can dance between them all throughout a single day. Practice being aware of your feminine divine nature and step fully into that power.

8. Take Mental Break Days

> *I take mental break days so that I don't*
> *have a mental break down.*
> —Cultivating Radiance

Have you ever had one of those days (maybe a week?) where you've run from one thing to another without pausing to breathe? Mental break days are an antidote to our sometimes-insane schedules and are vital to our creativity, passion, and turning up our radiance.

It starts with a compelling vision.

First, take a few minutes to close your eyes and dream about your perfect day of bliss. Where would you be? What would you be doing? How would your body and mind feel?

Next, create the space.

Choose a day and plan to take that entire day off. Enlist help for kids, pets, and work. Make necessary arrangements: reservations for massages or meals, collecting art supplies, whatever is needed to create *your* day. Sometimes, I'll just grab food and my journal, and head out into the hills for hours of meditation and writing.

The whole point of a mental break day is to rejuvenate, reenergize, and bring balance back into your life. When will you take yours?

9. Play!

Let your five-year-old self out; stretch yourself to explore, play, and find the adventures in life. It might mean getting together with children and letting them remind you of what it is like to play. Put on fairy wings, dance with ribbons, squish your feet into the mud … do whatever it takes to wake up the light of youth.

Rather than thinking like a grown-up who knows everything, take a look at your life with fresh, childlike eyes. See things in nature, your home, work, or lover as if for the first time.

10. Serve and Be Well Used (in a Good Way)

By being completely grounded and sharing our radiance superpowers with a passion, we create artistry in our lives. When we serve from our heart, it brings our purpose to life. Doing anything from guilt or obligation is a drain. Stop it.

Look at what your unique offerings are and give yourself fully, no holding back. It sounds like it could be draining, but it is just the opposite.

Serving may come in the form of offering kind words, encouragement, compassion, understanding, or a hug. It may be spending time being present with another person or serving your community by sharing your talents or skills. Listen to your heart and you will know how best to serve.

Activate your divine feminine wisdom and purpose with joy and light, so at the end of the day, you will be able to lie in bed and think, "My gifts and talents were well-used today."

May you honor your teacher within, cultivate your radiance, and delight in the experience of the REAL Beautiful you!

Energy Healing Tips by Anne Catherine Morrison

Meeting Anne Catherine was another expression of how we are attracted to similar vibrations. As I was drenched in the study of energy medicine while writing this book, she was introduced to me by a good friend. I am honored to share some of her top secret energy healing tips to empower your life. With over twenty years of training and experience in energy healing—including healing touch therapy, Reiki, Reflexology, and kinesiology applications—she spreads her magic touch like ripples across the water to her clientele within her community, among friends, and intrinsically out to the universe at large. Anne Catherine is an energy healer living in Brampton, Ontario, and practices energy medicine from her Natural Healing Arts Centre (nhacentre.ca).

During any energy medicine technique, you are always encouraged to breathe in through the nose, retain the breath as long as you can without strain, and then slowly release the breath.

1. Soothe Premenstrual Syndrome (PMS)

Just above your outside ankle, place three fingers—index, middle, and ring finger—one above another with index finger closest to the knee and ring finger closest to the ankle bone and the middle finger sitting between these two fingers. Press and release this area below the fingers seven times while you breathe. Place three fingers—index, middle, and ring finger—on the area above the wrist on the palm side. Your index finger will rest closest to the elbow and your ring finger will sit just above where the wrist meets the hand. Press and release as above.

2. Soothe Headaches

Place right and left hand palm down on your thighs while standing—right hand to right thigh, left hand to left thigh. Firmly press the point where your middle finger reaches on each thigh. Press and release this point seven times.

3. Balance Irregularity

Vigorously rub and massage with your hands and fingers downward from the top of the outside thigh to the knee to encourage regularity. It is critically important that you find balance in this powerful system in your body so it can effectively release toxins and wastes.

4. Heal Colds and Increase Immunity

Drink a tall glass of water and then trace the kidney meridian line. Begin tracing just under the right collarbone (K27 as indicated in chapter 8) on the right side and follow a line down just to the right of the center of your chest to the groin. Continue down the inside of the right inner thigh and downward as you circle behind the ankle bone and then up the inside of the foot to the halfway point and then underneath the soles of the foot. Repeat on other side. Remember to follow the breath exercise related above. This technique draws energy from Father Sky to Mother Earth.

5. Calm Your Fears and Soothe Your Nervous System

Alternate holding each pinkie finger firmly to help bring a sense of peace and calm to your mind, body, and spirit. This technique is powerful under any circumstances that create fear, panic, or stress. It is very easy to do anywhere without anyone even knowing.

6. Soothe Abdominal Pain or Menstrual Cramps

Place the tips of your fingers from both hands along the center line of your scalp. Press your fingers along the center skull line and move them away from the center line with heavy pressure. Lift the fingers and place them further along the center line as you work to the back of the head and neck.

7. Release Neck and Shoulder Pain

Hold on to each earlobe with thumb and index finger and pull downward until finger and thumb slide off the ear. Re-place the index finger and thumb just above the earlobe and pull outward until thumb and finger leave the ear. Continue this pulling action on the ear as you work your way to the top of the ear.

8. Increase Metabolism/Weight Loss

Hold the three finger tips of the right hand —index, middle, and ring finger— just above the top center point on the collarbone in the indent that resides there at the front of the lower throat, while the same left fingertips gently press and hold a point on the temple by the hairline. Switch the right fingertips to the right temple and the left fingertips to the indent above the collarbone on the lower throat area and gently hold these points before switching them again. Repeat this sequence as you breathe in and out slowly for several minutes.

9. Improve Your Eyesight

Rub deeply under the center area of the collarbone while you alternate holding the right and left side of the navel point (belly button).

10. Relieve Hormonal Nausea and Motion Sickness

Place your three middle fingers crosswise just above the area where the wrist meets the palm side of the hand (your index finger will be closest to the elbow and your ring finger will be closest to the wrist). Press and lift these fingers off and on this area while you breathe slowly in and out through the nose for 3 minutes. Repeat on the other wrist.

Yoga for Beauty Tips by Gina Gallo

With her vast insight regarding the mind, body, and spirit (Hatha, Vinyasa, Ashtanga, Anusara, Yin, Restorative, Naam Yoga, reflexology, Qi-Gong, biometaphysical healing, and holistic nutrition), yoga expert and healing warrior Gina Gallo (paschima.com) gives us her most potent tips that shower our energy being with enough love, beauty, and healing to send our electromagnetic vibration to the heavens. Her rare and deep knowledge of the yogic sciences is truly a gift. Gina shares her top yoga and mudra wisdom with us to help speed up hormonal and total body balance, to induce healing from the inside out, and to unveil our self-love and peace within.

Mudra for Hormonal System Balance

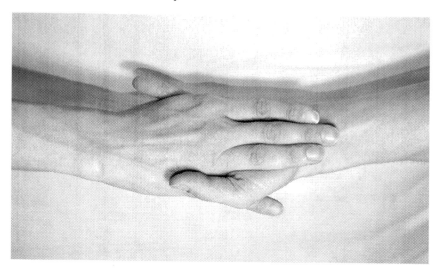

Technique:

1. Place right hand on top of left.

2. Separate pinkie fingers and thumbs and interlock them.

3. Let the index, middle, and ring fingers extend out to connect to wrists.

4. Set mudra at the level of the navel center.

Benefits:

- regulates hormonal systems
- improves lymphatic function
- alleviates headaches
- eases menopausal symptoms

Mudra for Total Body System Balance

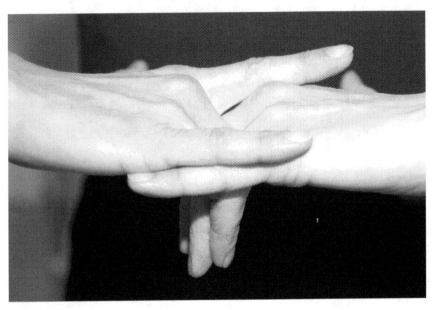

Technique:

1. Slide hands to connect, leaving the right index and pinkie fingers out to rest on top of left index and pinkie fingers.

2. Thumbs point toward chest, at level with heart line.

3. Middle and ring fingers extend and point down toward the earth.

Benefits:

- Balances the hormonal system
- balances the glandular system
- supports menopause

Self-Love Mudra

Technique:

1. Connect thumbs, index, and pinkie fingers.

2. Interlace middle and ring fingers.

3. Open palms, heels of hands separate.

4. Set mudra at the level of the heart line.

Benefits:

- cultivates self-love

- nourishes your being with love

Note: One can perform mudras while sitting, standing, lying down, or walking, at any time of the day. Mudras can be done as a meditation with long slow deep breathing or alone, as required.

Child's Pose: Garbhasana

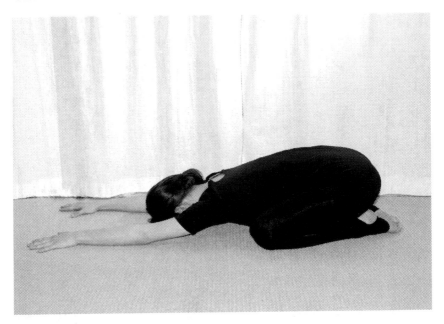

Technique:

1. Separate the knees as wide as the yoga mat, and bring the mounds of the big toes together.

2. Press the pelvis back toward the heels while lengthening the spine.

3. Rest arms alongside body comfortably, rest center of forehead on yoga mat.

4. Expand the breath into the back body and allow the breath to soften the muscles of the back and create a feeling of deep peace underneath the waves of the breath.

5. Breathe long, slow, deep breaths.

Benefits:

- massages the abdominal organs, kidneys, and adrenals
- relieves cramps and constipation

- promotes healing and relaxation to the entire body
- provides spinal integration and comfort to lower back

Downward Facing Dog: Adho-Mukha-Svanasana

Technique:

1. From a stable table pose, inhale to prepare, and then exhale, curling all the toes under and lifting the sit bones into the air, keeping the knees slightly bent and the heels up off the floor.

2. Lengthen through the arms and spine.

3. Keeping shoulders relaxed, draw the shoulder blades toward the pelvis.

4. Settle into a neutral position through your back and spine.

5. Stretch through the legs, and when comfortable, begin to straighten legs and lower heels toward the earth.

6. Find a balance point between the front of the body and the back of the body.

7. On an inhalation, draw energy up into the arms and legs. With each inhalation, allow this energy to radiate out, providing stability and support in the pose.

8. Settle deeper into the pose with each conscious breath and allow deep stillness to bathe the nervous system.

9. Hold and breathe for five full breaths. This pose can also be held for 3-5 minutes.

Benefits:
- calms the brain and nervous system
- alleviates mild depression
- energizes the body
- reduces menstrual irritations
- creates integration and balance between the upper body and lower body
- strengthens and stretches legs and shoulders

Seated Spinal Twist: Ardha Matsyendrasana

Technique:

1. Begin in a simple crossed-legged seated position with the right leg in front. Press the sit bones into the earth and lengthen up through the torso, lifting the rib cage evenly from all four sides, as you relax the shoulders and draw the shoulder blades down the back.

2. Place the sole of the right foot to the floor outside the left knee and slide the left heel to touch the right hip.

3. Press firmly into the right sole of the foot and exhale to twist toward the right thigh. Place the right palm on the floor or a prop behind and close to the center of the body.

4. Place the left hand, elbow, or crook of elbow to the outside of the right knee.

5. Turn the head to look over the right shoulder, with the chin parallel to the earth.

6. Inhale and continue to lengthen up through the spine; exhale to deepen the rotation without force or strain.

Benefits:
- massages the digestive organs for proper functioning
- stimulates the immune system and lymph flow
- sedates the nervous system
- energizes the spine, opens the rib cage and breath
- stimulates ovaries and pancreas

Bridge Pose: Setu Bandha Sarvangasana

Technique:
1. Lie on the back with knees bent, feet hip-width apart, ankles directly under knees, and arms alongside the body.

2. Move into bridge pose: inhale and scoop the tailbone under, maintain the tuck of the pelvis, press firmly into the feet, and lift the torso up off the earth, keeping arms alongside the body for support. Optional to clasp hands underneath to hold bridge pose.

3. Keep legs activated by hugging the muscles around the bones on all four sides to support the knees.

4. Lengthen the back body as well as the front body, creating space between the vertebrae as you press the knees and the chest away from each other.

5. Expand the entire chest cavity and create space between the ribs, expanding the breath, freeing the diaphragm, and massaging the heart.

Benefits:

- stretches the spine
- strengthens the back, buttock, legs, and ankles
- opens the chest, solar plexus, and hips
- massages the kidneys, thyroid, and adrenal glands
- improves digestion

Squat: Malasana

Technique:

1. Begin in Tadasana, hands in prayer mudra. Maintaining a neutral spine, rise up onto the toes and bend the knees to descend slowly. Feel the tailbone being pulled straight down toward the earth.

2. Come into a squat by lowering your heels to the floor or on a prop.

3. With hands in prayer mudra, press the arms out against the knees and the knees inward against the arms.

4. Feel a tremendous release downward through the pelvic floor as the entire pelvis and abdomen are massaged, and opened toward the earth.

5. Draw the inhalation into the pelvis and exhale downward and out. Hold for at least five breaths.

Benefits:

- massages all the abdominal and reproductive organs
- opens the hips and groin

Seated Forward Bend: Paschimottanasana

Technique:

1. Begin in *Dandasana* (seated position with the legs extended forward) feet flexed.

2. Hinge forward at the hips and walk the hands down your legs, maintaining a flat back.

3. Rest with the hands alongside the legs for five breaths. Lengthen the torso with each inhalation and allow the torso

to descend with each exhalation, maintaining the spine in a neutral position.

4. Walk the hands back up the legs returning to *Dandasana* slowly, and with control.

Benefits:

- traction and lengthening of the spine
- stimulates adrenals, pancreas, and ovaries
- relief of menopausal and menstrual symptoms
- aids digestion
- creates full breathing for back lungs
- is therapeutic for infertility, insomnia, and high blood pressure

Deep Relaxation: Savasana

Technique:

1. Begin by lying comfortably on the back. Close the eyes and rest the spine.

2. Lift the flesh of the buttocks out toward the heels, lengthen through the legs, and let the feet fall out to the sides.

3. Release the shoulders away from the ears and slide the shoulder blades under the back.

4. Lengthen and rest the arms alongside the body at a forty-five-degree angle with palms facing up.

5. Sense a natural intelligence and interconnectedness of all the body systems.

6. Feel the body come into stillness and the muscles release and relax away from the bones. Feel the joints open up as gravity moves through the body.

7. Scan the body and consciously invite each part to relax more deeply. Continue to feel the ebb and flow of the breath, while the body-mind integrates to the experience of unity and interconnectedness.

8. Continue to breathe consciously and bathe in this feeling of deep peace, stillness, and harmony.

9. Remain in *Savasana* for at least twenty minutes.

10. Come out completely drenched in a feeling of surrender and balance. Gradually bring movement back into each body part. Bend the knees and roll to the right. Use the hands to support the transition to an upright position.

11. Allow a feeling of gratitude, love, and deep relaxation to saturate your entire being.

Benefits:

- sedates and relaxes the body and mind
- soothes the nervous system

- calms the brain, reduces fatigue, and helps to lower blood pressure
- initiates a feeling of deep peace, stillness, and relaxation

Finding Beauty Tips by Fred Connors

I came to know Fred Connors when he starred in the inspiring television show X-Weighted as a self-esteem expert and a skilled makeover artist. I was inspired by his insight and ability to carry the participants on the show past their fears to uncover and embrace their own real beauty. His insight and desire to help women feel beautiful led to the development of FRED. face, a universal cosmetic line that helps to simplify beauty for all ages and skin types. He extended his understanding of beauty even further when he brought food, beauty, and art together in his salon, café, and art gallery in Halifax, Nova Scotia. Understanding beauty from the inside out is Fred's business, and he invites us to include affordable luxury in our lives to honor and celebrate who we really are. I am excited to experience this in "Fred style" the next time I visit his hometown. Get connected to Fred and more beauty on his website at fredstyle.ca.

1. Always remember that "pretty" is something you put on; beautiful is something you already are. Beauty is not about being perfect; it is who we are and how we live in this world.

2. Take control of what you can immediately. There are lots of things that don't take a lot of time and effort to achieve that can make you feel better. Sleeping in a freshly cleaned bedroom feels beautiful. Do it every day.

3. Beauty is expressed in how we relate to those around us, how we treat people, what we eat, and how we live. The world is

filled with pretty people who do not demonstrate beauty in their actions.

4. Take time to realize that above all else, you matter. Indulge in an activity that will bring value to your everyday life. Treat yourself to a pedicure even if you have to budget for it.

5. Returning at the end of a day to a clean and organized home allows you to enter a peaceful surrounding you enjoy being in. When our personal space is welcoming and free of things to do, it allows for a space that promotes wellness, which is a huge part of feeling beautiful.

6. Every day, do something that leaves a positive impact, even if it is toward only one person. At the end of the day, if you haven't made even a small difference, it is not yet time to go to bed.

7. Get over yourself. Stop focusing on everything that is wrong with you or your life and realize that compared to someone else's situation, you have nothing to complain about.

8. Make a powerful first impression. Starting a conversation by complimenting someone else inspires confidence. Focusing on your faults when meeting someone causes them to lose interest in anything great about you that may exist.

9. We are all born into this world equally beautiful. Think of a time you felt whole, valued, and appreciated. This is what makes you beautiful, and it exists every day even if you have forgotten it is there.

10. Constantly be inspired by others. Being open to the beauty that exists in others will allow you to build a stronger sense of your own potential. Potential is greater beauty yet to be discovered.

Finding Comfort and Balance Tips by G. Brian Benson

From the first moment I listened to Brian's insight, it was his comforting and balanced wisdom that spoke to me. I believe it is the simplest of wisdom and the voice inside of us that contains the power to uncover the secrets of who we really are. Brian reminds us of this in the tips below and is a living example that we can achieve much more than we ever realized when we are guided by them. He's a multiple-award-winning self-help author and filmmaker, a coach, speaker, actor, musician, workshop facilitator, published children's author, and inspirational poet who has finished over fifty triathlons—including four Ironman distance races. He's also completely committed to helping others become the best they can be. Learn more about Brian on his website at gbrianbenson.com.

1. *Meditate.* As Cindy guides in great depth in this book, I agree that meditation is the place where we can connect to spirit and hear divine wisdom. Find the best combination of meditations that work for you. Being consistent with your practice increases your results. A powerful meditation I recommend outside of this book is "Manifest Your Destiny" by Dr. Wayne Dyer.

2. *Give Thanks.* Giving thanks for what we have is probably the single most important thing that we can do for ourselves. It puts us in a positive frame of mind and lets the universe know that we are open to receiving more.

3. *Exercise Daily.* Moving or exercising your body every day is necessary to keep the natural flow of energy inside of us balanced and powerful. When you move your body, you balance your weight, reduce your stress, think more clearly,

feel better about yourself, and stay productive in your life. Try out various forms of exercise and find the ones that work for you, and then make them a part of your day. The key is to make whatever you do a habit. Once again, the consistent performance of exercise and movement empowers our living and being to higher levels, guaranteed.

4. ***Laugh.*** Laughter really is the best medicine! As E. E. Cummings wrote, "The most wasted of all days is one without laughter." How could we not agree? To laugh is to feel alive. To laugh with others is to be spiritually connected with them. Laughter brings hope. Laughter brings relief. Laughter heals our bodies. Laughter brings people together. Your quality of life will instantly improve!

5. ***Declutter.*** Stuff has a way of creeping into our lives, and before we know it, it starts to take over! Unfinished projects are like taunting specters grabbing a hold of our sanity. They cling to us, weigh us down, and evaporate our energy. When we find ways to let go of unwanted stuff and complete unfinished projects, we begin to feel lighter and more balanced, symbolizing the freedom we create as we declutter our lives on all levels.

6. ***Do What You Love.*** Are you doing what you love? This top-ten tip is really as simple as it sounds. If you aren't doing what you love, start making it happen. Watch what happens to your life when you do. Your world will come alive. You will feel happier and more fulfilled and will begin living on purpose.

7. ***Treat Yourself with Respect.*** Every negative word spoken quietly inside your mind is a seed that builds the patterns of thinking, believing, and living in the external world. Negative thoughts breed negative thinking and patterns,

while positive and respectful thoughts create the opposite. Love and respect who you are, and watch your confidence and well-being soar.

8. ***Listen to Your Heart.*** Let your mind rest, and let your heart take over. Listening to your heart works in all facets of your life—a positive or negative feeling you get about a person you just met, whether or not you want to take a particular job you are offered, or feelings you are having dealing with your boyfriend or girlfriend. Honoring your feelings isn't always the easiest route to take or the most popular. But I can tell you it is always the right route. Being honest with yourself is the most important thing you can do.

9. ***Go for a Walk.*** Want to clear your head? Want to reconnect with yourself? Want to get your creative juices flowing? Want to change your attitude? Want to give your body a little exercise? Want to get in touch with nature? Want to relieve some stress? Want to connect with a friend? Go for a walk! It is such a powerful cure-all, and it's free! I can't tell you how many times I have gone for a walk and felt totally rejuvenated during and after it. It's a fantastic way to get unstuck and wake your senses back up.

10. ***Leave Ten Minutes Early.*** How often do you find yourself rushing to work or someplace else that you need to be? How does it make you feel? Stressed? Angry? Guilty? You know there is a very simple way to eliminate all those unwanted feelings that come from being rushed. Why not try leaving 10 minutes early? I realize that we occasionally run late because of reasons out of our control, but the majority of the time, it doesn't have to be that way. Why not head out the door a few minutes earlier than usual? You would be amazed at how peaceful and restful your drive into work can be. If you

miss a traffic light, it becomes no big deal. If you get stuck at a railroad crossing, same thing—no big deal. Knowing that you have a few extra minutes will help you relax and make your commute so much smoother, easier, and less stressful. When I started leaving ten minutes early to go to work, I noticed the difference immediately. I arrived at work feeling so much more peaceful and balanced. I was ready to start the day. So if you can allow yourself those ten extra minutes, you will feel at ease during your commute, and you will arrive at your destination in a much better mood, feeling very balanced and centered.

Fear-to-Faith Tips by Christine Arylo

When I synchronously came to know Christine Arylo, I celebrated her efforts to pave a much-needed pathway to self-love. Her passion to bring focus to one of the greatest healing secrets, gives women the permission to love themselves better. Christine is an inspirational catalyst and internationally recognized speaker and best-selling author who teaches people how to put their most important partnership first—the one with themselves—so that they can create the life their hearts and souls crave. The popular author of the go-to book on relationships *Choosing ME Before WE* and the self-love handbook *Madly in Love with ME: the Daring Adventure to Becoming Your Own Best Friend*, she's affectionately known as the Queen of Self-Love. Christine founded the International Day of Self-Love on February 13 and is the cofounder of the self-love and empowerment school for women, Inner Mean Girl Reform School. For more about Christine, visit her websites at ChristineArylo.com and ChooseSelfLove.com.

Release Your Faith in Fear and Embrace Your Faith in Love

Here is the truth: everyone faces fear. Being fearless isn't about not having fear, it's about looking fear in the face and saying, "Yeah, I see you. Yeah, you freak me out. And so what? I am moving forward anyway!" Fearlessness is all about choosing courage of the heart over contraction in the heart. Contraction happens when we pull away from love—connection, support, truth—and as a result find ourselves feeling isolated, confused, and defeated. Courage, on the other hand comes, from the expanded heart, where at the core beats the most powerful force in the world: love.

As the co-creator, with Gabrielle Bernstein, of the Forty-Day Fear Cleanse (theFearCleanse.com), I know that the best time to cut fear off at the pass is to deal with it right as it emerges. This way it doesn't have too long to stew in the dark, where it can feed on your avoidance, pain, shame, and procrastination and grow to superhuman proportions. The key is to learn how to shift your faith in fear into faith in love.

Sometimes it can be challenging in the moment to switch your mind from fear to faith. When fear is all up in your business, you feel frozen, full of anxiety, overwrought with self-doubt, or just plain crabby. The *last* thing you want to do when you are in the midst of a fear attack is to attune to love. You are too gnarled up in your nasty but comfortable "fear blankey." But turning to love in these moments is the only chance you've got to realign your mind and move forward in the direction that leads you to the happiness your heart and soul desire.

Inspired by the Forty-Day Fear Cleanse, here are three ways you can turn your faith in fear into faith in love and move yourself toward what truly makes you happy.

1. ***Get naked with your fear.*** Pull you fear out of the closet and look at it up close for exactly what it is. Make one big fear

list with the header, "I am afraid that ..." List all the things you can think of that you are afraid of. Take your list to your bathtub, fill the bath with good salts, get naked, climb in, and then read the letter out loud: "I am afraid that ..." Really let yourself feel it, releasing the fear into the salt bath, until you are complete. Then dissolve the list into the salt water, pull the plug, and watch it go down the drain. Rinse. Dry off. Write the words, "I choose to have faith in love" on your body with eyeliner or lip liner. Go to sleep clean and clear, knowing you were courageous enough to get naked with your fear and make the choice to choose love. And that, in itself, offers a big release.

2. **Connect with someone who really knows you and laugh, hard.** Fear is like having congested lungs. It gets all caught up inside and you just need to get it out! This one is inspired by my friend and founder of the feminine leadership nonprofit Shakti Rising, Shannon Thompson. She says when she's in a fear pretzel, she calls up someone who knows her super well and spills the beans on all the crazy stuff fear has got going through her brain. You know, like a mad woman fear ramble, where you can ask the craziest questions that fear has planted in your head. You then ask your friend to 1. Tell you the truth and 2. Help you see how crazy fear has got you thinking. In the process, you can bet that you will end with a big laugh, and you will cough out fear like yesterday's cold.

3. **Go talk to the big guns.** When fear is staring you down, that is the moment you've got to drop to your knees and make a collect-call 911 to a higher force than you or fear—and there is only one number to dial, and that is God. Call it the divine, the universe, source, Gaia, whatever—just stop, drop, and connect into something bigger than you that never loses faith,

only offers it. One of the most effective ways I have found to do this in the moment is to use one of the most powerful love mantras I know. Think of a love mantra like a divine Tic Tac, as in Tic Tacs turn sour breath into fresh breath, and love mantras turn fear into love. In the moment, as you feel fear staring you down, stop, close your eyes, breathe, and repeat this love mantra over and over again until you feel fear release and faith restore itself: "I choose to release my faith in fear. I choose to have faith in love."

REAL Beautiful Words

Kind words are a creative force, a power that concurs in the building up
of all that is good, and energy that showers blessings upon the world.
—Lawrence G. Lovasik, Clergyman

Words are the keys to the heart.
—Chinese proverb

I Am Real Beautiful by Colleen Sidun

This song was created for my REAL Beautiful Movement to inspire women of all ages to see the truth and power in who they really are. I thank Colleen Sidun for lending her talent and beautiful voice for this cause. You can listen to this song and join the REAL Beautiful Movement at realbeautiful.ca.

I Am REAL Beautiful
Written and performed by Colleen Sidun

When I look in the mirror
Sometimes I don't know who I see
Is that me?

My God it's been some time
She looks honest, true, and kind
Is that mine?

The memories flash before my eyes
And I realize
I've been blind ...

(Chorus)
Cause I am REAL Beautiful
Inside out
I am REAL Beautiful
And there's no doubt
I am REAL Beautiful
Yes I am.

Yes I am.
Amen!

If you look closer at me
You'll see my heart is open wide
Just come inside.

And if you can truly see me
For who I really am
I'd say, Amen.

Some might try to hurt me
And make me feel the fool
But I won't let them change me
Cause I've realized
I'm not blind.

(Chorus)

So when you look in that mirror
Make sure you see just who's inside
Now don't you hide
Be honest, true, and kind
Say what's on your mind
Now don't be shy.

Let the memories pass before your eyes
And realize you're not blind.

(Chorus)

The Manifesto of Encouragement
by Danielle Laporte

Author and inspirational speaker Danielle Laporte, who writes weekly at her website daniellelaporte.com, shares this call to action for those who need hope and inspiration to carry them through the day.

There are Tibetan Buddhist monks in a temple in the Himalayas endlessly reciting mantras for the cessation of your suffering and for the flourishing of your happiness.

Someone you haven't met yet is already dreaming of adoring you.

Someone is writing a book that you will read in the next two years that will change how you look at life.

Nuns in the Alps are in endless vigil, praying for the Holy Spirit to alight the hearts of all of God's children.

A farmer is looking at his organic crops and whispering, "Nourish them."

Someone wants to kiss you, to hold you, to make tea for you. Someone is willing to lend you money, wants to know what your favorite food is, and treat you to a movie. Someone in your orbit has something immensely valuable to give you—for free.

Something is being invented this year that will change how your generation lives, communicates, heals, and passes on.

The next great song is being rehearsed.

Thousands of people are in yoga classes right now intentionally sending light out from their heart chakras and wrapping it around the earth.

Millions of children are assuming that everything is amazing and will always be that way.

Someone is in profound pain, and a few months from now, they'll be thriving like never before. They just can't see it from where they're at.

Someone who is craving to be partnered, to be acknowledged, to *arrive*, will get precisely what is desired—and even more. And because that gift will be so fantastical in its reach and sweetness, it will quite magically alter the memory of angsty longing and render it all "so worth the wait."

Someone has recently cracked open their joyous, genuine nature because they did the hard work of hauling years of oppression off of their psyche—this luminous juju is floating in the ether, and is accessible to you.

Someone just this second wished for world peace, in earnest.

Someone is fighting the fight so that you don't have to.

Some civil servant is making sure that you get your mail, and your garbage is picked up, that the trains are running on time, and that you are generally safe. Someone is dedicating their days to protecting your civil liberties and clean drinking water.

Someone is regaining sanity. Someone is coming back from the dead. Someone is genuinely forgiving the seemingly unforgivable. Someone is curing the incurable.

You. Me. Some. One. Now.

> Consider that you radiate. At all times consider that what you're feeling right now is rippling outward into a field of is-ness that anyone can dip their oar into. You are felt. You are heard. You are seen. If you were not here, the world would be different. Because of your presence, the universe is expanding.
> —Danielle Laporte

Resources

Cindy Heath

www.realbeautiful.ca

When you join the REAL Beautiful Movement you stay connected to the ongoing gifts, insights, and secrets shared directly in your email in-box. You receive you own sparkling heart download, so you can make your heart sparkle and share it with someone else! Share the mystical power contained in the healing mantra card as a beautiful gift for any occasion; to saturate your being with healing, love and abundance or give this experience to the special women on your gift list. Place the card on the tables or in the gift bags at healing retreats/ conferences to raise the vibrational energy of the group. Take part in the online healing experience through the *Forty Day REAL Beautiful Sacred Sadhana* available, or set up a phone/Skype counseling session to get you started on your path to higher vibrations that bring the miracles you wish for, and keep your energy vibrations high with the magic power contained within the upcoming *Gratitude and Self-Love*

App available soon for download. I am offering a treasure chest full of ways for us to keep staying REAL Beautiful together! Sat Nam.

Kristine Carlson

www.kristinecarlson.com

Look for these books by Kristine Carlson:

- *Don't Sweat the Small Stuff for Moms*
- *Don't Sweat the Small Stuff for Women*
- *Don't Sweat the Small Stuff in Love*
- *Heartbroken Open*

  In memory of the healing perspectives brought to the world by Richard Carlson (May 16, 1961- December 13, 2006)

- *An Hour to Live, an Hour to Love by Richard Carlson*
- *Don't Sweat the Small Stuff: And It is all Small Stuff by Richard Carlson*
- *Don't Sweat the Small Stuff for Teens by Richard Carlson*

Dr. Wayne Dyer

www.drwaynedyer.com

Look for these books, CDs, and DVDs available now by Dr. Wayne Dyer:

- *Real Magic: Creating Miracle in Everyday Life*
- *Your Sacred Self*
- *Pulling Your Own Strings*

- *I Am Wishes Fulfilled Meditation*
- *Secrets for Manifesting*
- *The Shift*
- *Wishes Fulfilled*
- *Experiencing the Miraculous*
- *I Can See Clearly Now*
- *Your Erroneous Zones*
- *Excuses Begone*
- *Change Your Thoughts Change Your Life*
- *Living the Wisdom of the Tao*
- *The Invisible Force*

Gregg Braden

www.greggbraden.com

Look for these books, CDs, and DVDs by Gregg Braden:

- *The Isaiah Effect*
- *Fractal Time*
- *Deep Truth*
- *The Spontaneous Healing of Belief*
- *The God Code*
- *Secrets of the Lost Mode of Prayer*
- *The Divine Matrix*
- *Entanglement*
- *The Science of Miracles*
- *Zero Point*

- *An Ancient Magical Prayer*
- *The Divine Name: Sounds of the God Code*

Donna Eden

www.innersource.net

Look for these books, CDs, and DVDs by Donna Eden:

- *The Little Book of Energy Medicine*
- *Energy Medicine*
- *Energy Medicine for Women*
- *The Energies of Love*
- *The Promise of Energy Psychology*

Dr. Rangie Singh

7th Dimension Health at www.7dhealth.com

Look for this book by Dr. Ranjie Singh:

- *Self-Healing: Powerful Techniques*

Yogi Bhajan

www.kundaliniresearchinstitute.com

Look for these books by Yogi Bhajan

- *The Chakras*
- *Foods for Health and Healing*

- *Transformations: Seeds of Change for the Aquarian Age Mastering the Self*
- *Mining Your Hidden Treasures*
- *I am Women Creative Sacred and Invincible*
- *Transformations Volume Two: Serving the Infinite*
- *Mind and Meditation*

References

Chapter 2

Dyer, Wayne W. 1978. *Pulling Your Own Strings.* HarperCollins: New York.

Dyer, Wayne W. 1992. *Real Magic: Creating Miracles in Everyday Life.* New York: HarperCollins.

Dyer, Wayne W. 2004. *The Power of Intention.* Hay House: Carlsbad CA: United States.

Chapter 3, 4

Derenne, Jennifer L., and Eugene V. Beresin. 2006. "Body Image, Media, and Eating Disorders." *Academic Psychiatry* 30 (May/June): 257–261.

Dispensa, Joe. 2007. *Evolve Your Brain: The Science of Changing Your Mind.* Deerfield Beach, FL: Health Communications Incorporated.

Dyer, Wayne W. 1992. *Real Magic: Creating Miracles in Everyday Life.* New York: HarperCollins.

Etcoff, Nancy, Susie Orbach, and Jennifer Scott. 2005. "Beyond Stereotypes: Rebuilding the Foundation of Beauty Beliefs." Dove Global Study White Paper.

Hawkins, David R. 2001. *Power vs. Force: The Hidden Determinants of Human Behavior.* Sedona, AZ: Veritas Publishing.

Hawkins, Nicole, P. Scott Richards, H. Mac Granley, and David M. Stein. 2004. "The Impact of Exposure to the Thin-Ideal Media Image on Women." *Eating Disorders* 12, no. 1: 35–50.

Kilbourne, Jean. 1995. *Slim Hope: Advertising and the Obsession with Slimness.* DVD.

Leaf, Caroline. 2009. *The Gift in You: Discover New Life Through Gifts Hidden In Your Mind.* South Lake, TX: Inprov.

Lipton, Bruce. 2005. *The Biology of Our Beliefs: Unleashing the Power of Consiouness, Matter, and Miracles.* Santa Rosa, CA: Mountain of Love/Elite Books.

Mowry, Scott. "Dr. David R. Hawkins—Measuring the Scale of Human Consciousness." *Miracles and Inspiration.* http://miraclesandinspiration.com/davidhawkins.html.

Wolf, Naomi. 2002. *The Beauty Myth: How Images of Beauty Are Used Against Women.* New York: Harper Perennial.

Yamamiya, Yuko, Thomas F. Cash, Susan E. Melnyk, Heidi D. Posavac, and Steven S. Posavac. 2005. "Women's Exposure to Thin-and-Beautiful Media Images: Body Image Effects of Media-Ideal Internalization and Impact-Reduction Interventions." *Body Image* 2, no. 1 (March): 74–80.

Chapters 5, 6, and 7

Caprio, Frank, and Joseph R. Berger. 1998. *Healing Yourself with Self-Hypnosis.* Revised by Caroline Miller. New York: Prentice Hall.

Carr, Kris. 2011. *Crazy Sexy Diet: Eat Your Veggies, Ignite Your Spark, and Live Like You Mean It!* Guilford, CT: Globe Pequot Press.

Carr, Kris. 2012. *Crazy Sexy Kitchen: 150 Plant-Empowered Recipes to Ignite a Mouthwatering Revolution*. Carlsbad, CA: Hay House

Co, Stephen, and Eric B. Robins with John Merryman. 2002. *Your Hands Can Heal You: Pranic Healing Energy Remedies to Boost Vitality and Speed Recovery from Common Health Problems*. New York: Simon and Schuster.

Dyer, Wayne W. 1992. *Real Magic: Creating Miracles in Everyday Life*. New York: HarperCollins.

Hawkins, David R. 2001. *Power vs. Force: The Hidden Determinants of Human Behavior*. Sedona, AZ: Veritas Publishing.

Chapter 8

Eden, Donna. 2008. *Energy Medicine for Women: Aligning Your Body's Energies to Boost Your Health and Vitality*. New York: Penguin Group.

Chapter 9

Carroll, Cain, and Revital Carroll. 2012. *Mudras of India: A Comprehensive Guide to the Hand Gestures of Yoga and Indian Dance*. London: Singing Dragon.

Gray-Davidson, Frena. 2000. *Ayurvedic Healing*. Twin Lakes, Wisconsin: Lotus Press.

Hunt, Mary. *Opening Chapter Quote*. http://www.lookforthelight.com/

Tiwari, Maya. 2000. *The Path of Practice: A Woman's Book of Healing with Food, Breath and Sound*. New York: Ballantine Books.

Chapter 10

Doabia, Harbans Sing. 2007. *Sacred Nitnem*. Amritsar, India: Singh Brothers.

Dyer, Wayne W. 1992. *Real Magic: Creating Miracles in Everyday Life*. New York: HarperCollins.

Funk, Robert W., and Roy W. Hoover. 1993. *The Five Gospels: What Did Jesus Really Say? The Search for the Authentic Words of Jesus.* Toronto: Maxwell Macmillan Canada.

Holy Bible New Revised Standard Version: Catholic Edition (NRSV). 1991. Ottawa, Canada: Catholic Bible Press, Thomas Nelson Publishers.

Meyer, Marvin. 1992. *The Gospel of St. Thomas: The Hidden Sayings of Jesus,* second edition. New York: HarperCollins.

The Good News Bible: Today's English Version. Toronto: The Canadian Bible Society.

Yogi Bhajan. 2007. *The Aquarian Teacher: KRI International Kundalini Yoga Teacher Training Textbook Level One Instructor.* Santa Cruz, NM: Kundalini Research Institute.

Chapter 11

Dyer, Wayne W. 1992. *Real Magic: Creating Miracles in Everyday Life.* New York: HarperCollins.

St. Therese of Lisieux. 1957. *The Story of a Soul: The Autobiography of St. Therese of Lisieux. New York, NY: Doubleday*

Wilson, Edward O. 1984. *Biophilia.* Cambridge, MA: The President and Fellows of Harvard College.

Chapter 12

Braden, Gregg. 2001. *Beyond Zero Point: The Journey to Compassion.* DVD. Louisville, CO: Gaiam.

Braden, Gregg. 2006. *Secrets of the Lost Mode of Prayer: The Hidden Power of Beauty, Blessing, Wisdom, and Hurt.* Carlsbad, CA: Hay House.

Braden, Gregg. 2000. *The Isaiah Effect: Lost Science of Prayer and Prophecy.* New York: Three Rivers Press.

Braden, Gregg. 2009. *The Science of Miracles: The Quantum Launguage of Healing, Peace, Feeling, and Belief.* DVD. Carlsbad, CA: Hay House.

Braden, Gregg. 2008. *The Spontaneous Healing of Belief: Shattering the Paradigms of False Limits*. Carlsbad, CA: Hay House.

Braden, Gregg. 2009. *Walking Between the Worlds: Understanding the Inner Technologies of Emotion*. DVD. Louisville, CO: Gaiam Americas.

Chopra, Deepak, and Gregg Braden. 2006. *An Ancient Magical Prayer: Insights from the Dead Sea Scrolls*. Audiobook. Carlsbad, CA: Hay House.

Chapter 13

Braden, Gregg. 2008. The Spontaneous Healing of Belief: Shattering the Paradigms of False Limits. Hay House: United States

Dale, Cyndi. 2009. *The Complete Book of Chakra Healing: Activate the Transformative Power of Your Energy Centers*. Woodbury, MN: Llewellyn Publications.

Hirschi, Gertrud. 2000. *Mudras: Yoga in Your Hands*. San Francisco: Red Wheel/Weiser LLC.

Khalsa, Guru Dharam S., and Darryl O'Keefe. 2002. *The Kundalini Yoga Experience: Bringing Body, Mind, and Spirit Together*. New York: Simon and Schuster.

Servan-Schreiber, David. 2004. *The Instinct to Heal: Curing Depression, Anxiety, and Stress Without Drugs and Without Talk Therapy*. Emmaus, PA: Rodale Books.

Chapter 14

Alypsis Inc. http://www.alypsis.ca.

Bach Original Flower Remedies. http://www.bachremedies.com.

Bailey Essences. http://www.baileyessences.com.

Cram, Jeffrey R. "A Convergence of Evidence: Flower Essence Therapy in the Treatment of Major Depression." *Calix* 1: 89. http://www.flowersociety.org/depression-study.pdf.

Flower Essence Society. http://www.flowersociety.org.

Olive, Barbra. 2007. *The Flower Healer*. New York: Cico Books.

The Bach Centre. http://www.bachcentre.com.

Chapter 15

Barrett, Sondra. 2013. *The Secret Secrets of Your Cells. Discovering Your Body's Inner Intelligence*. Sounds True, Inc: Boulder, CO.

Khalsa, Shakti Parwha Kaur. 1996. *Kundalini Yoga: The Flow of Eternal Power: A Simple Guide to the Yoga of Awareness*. New York: Berkley.

Singh, Ranjie. 1998. *Self-Healing Powerful Techniques*. Canada: Health Psychology Associates.

Tiwari, Maya. 2000. *The Path of Practice: A Woman's Book of Healing with Food, Breath and Sound*. New York: Ballantine Books.

Chapter 16

Atkinson, William Walker, and Lon Milo Duquette. 2012. *The Hindu Yogi Science of Breath*. San Francisco: Red Wheel/Weiser LLC.

Khalsa, Dharma Singh, and Cameron Stauth. 2011. *Meditation as Medicine: Activate the Power of Your Natural Healing Force*. New York: Simon and Schuster.

Chapter 17Eden, Donna. 2008. *Energy Medicine for Women: Aligning Your Body's Energies to Boost Your Health and Vitality*. New York: Penguin Group.

Fogarty, Carole. 2009. "12 Great Reasons to Start Alternate Nostril Breathing." *Rejuvenation Lounge*. http://thehealthylivinglounge. com/2009/06/16/12-great-reasons-to-start-alternate-nostril-breathing-today/.

Kater, Peter, and Snatam Kaur. 2012. *Heart of the Universe*. Kater Music/ BMI and Spirit Voyage Publishing.

Keller, Britt. 2012. "The Pineal Gland: A Link to Our Third Eye." *Brain World*. http://brainworldmagazine.com/ the-pineal-gland-a-link-to-our-third-eye/

Kjellgren, Anette, Sven Å Bood, Kajsa Axelsson, Torsten Norlander, and Fahri Saatcioglu. 2007. "Wellness Through a Comprehensive Yogic Breathing Program—a Controlled Pilot Trial." *BMC Complementary and Alternative Medicine* (December): 7(1):43.

Kochupillai, V., P. Kumar, D. Singh, D. Aggarwal, N. Bhardwaj, M. Bhutani, S. N. Das. 2005. "Effect of Rhythmic Breathing on Immune Functions and Tobacco Addiction." *Annals of the New York Academy of Sciences* 1056 (November): 242–52.

"Nadi (Yoga): Ida, Pingala and Sushumna." *Wikipedia.* http://en.wikipedia. org/wiki/Nadi_(yoga)#Ida.2C_Pingala_and_Sushumna.

"Nadis." *TheSecretsofYoga.com.* http://www.thesecretsofyoga.com/ kundalini-yoga-nadis.html.

Novotny, Sarah, and Len Kravitz. "The Science of Breathing." *The University of New Mexico.* http://www.unm.edu/~lkravitz/ Article%20folder/Breathing.html.

Singh, Indra. 2010. "Breathing Your Way to Health." *Natural Life*, no. 135 (September/October): 36–37.

Singh, Ranjie. 1998. *Self-Healing Powerful Techniques.* Canada: Health Psychology Associates.

"Studies Show Benefits of Controlled Breathing to Mind and Body." *SMU News Center.* http://smu.edu/experts/pitches/breathing-research.asp.

"The Science of Breath." *World Research Foundation.* http://www.wrf.org/ alternative-therapies/science-of-breath.php.

"Ujjayi (Victorious) Breath." *Yoga with Subhash.* http://yogawithsubhash. com/2010/08/07/ujjayi-victorious-breath/.

Yogi Bhajan. "From the Source—Victory!" *Kundalini Yoga.* December 1, 1992. http://www.3ho.org/ecommunity/2012/06/ from-the-source-victory/.

Yogi Bhajan. 2007. *The Aquarian Teacher: KRI International Kundalini Yoga Teacher Training Textbook Level One Instructor.* Santa Cruz, NM: Kundalini Research Institute.

Yogi Ramacharaka. 2009. *The Hindu-Yogi Science of Breath.* http://www. hermetics.org/pdf/ScienceOfBreath.pdf.

Dartmouth Correspondent. "The Real Meaning of 'Asan' and 'Praanayam'." Class Notes from a *Kriyayoga Session*. *http://www.kriyayoga-yogisatyam.org/Articles/AasanPranayam.pdf*

Chapter 18

Fahmi, Les, and Jim Robbins. 2007. *The Open-Focus Brain: Harnessing the Power of Attention to Heal Mind and Body*. Boston: Trumpeter Books

Khalsa, Dharma Singh, and Cameron Stauth. 2011. *Meditation as Medicine: Activate the Power of Your Natural Healing Force*. New York: Simon and Schuster.

Shannahoff-Khalsa, David. 2006. *Kundalini Yoga Meditation: Techniques Specific for Psychiatric Disorders, Couples Therapy, and Personal Growth*. New York: W. W. Norton and Company.

Yogi Bhajan. 2007. *The Aquarian Teacher: KRI International Kundalini Yoga Teacher Training Textbook Level One Instructor*. Santa Cruz, NM: Kundalini Research Institute.

Chapter 19

What is Kundalini Yoga quote. Yogi Bajan. 1997. *Aquarian Wisdom Calendar* 12/17/97. *The Power of Kundalini Yoga* quote. Yogi Bhajan, Ph. D. 2007. *The Aquarian Teacher: KRI International Kundalini Yoga Teacher Training Textbook Level One Instructor*. Kundalini Research Institute: Santa Cruz, N.M. *p. 20*

What is Kundalini Yoga. Khalsa, Shakti Parwha Kaur. 1996. *Kundalini Yoga: The Flow of Eternal Power. Berkeley Publishing Company: New York. pp. 11-12*

Sadhana quote. Yogi Bhajan, Ph. D. 2007. *The Aquarian Teacher: KRI International Kundalini Yoga Teacher Training Textbook Level One Instructor. Kundalini Research Institute: Santa Cruz, NM*. p. 144

The Science Behind Wearing a Head Cover. Yogi Bhajan, Ph. D. 2007. *The Aquarian Teacher: KRI International Kundalini Yoga Teacher Training Textbook Level One Instructor. Kundalini Research Institute: Santa Cruz, NM*. p. 151

Beauty Glands. Shakti Parwha Kaur Khalsa. 1996. Kundalini Yoga: The Flow of Eternal Power. The Berkley Publishing Company: New York. p. 240

Breath/Pranayama. Yogi Bhajan, Ph. D. 2007. *The Aquarian Teacher: KRI International Kundalini Yoga Teacher Training Textbook Level One Instructor. Kundalini Research Institute: Santa Cruz, NM.* p. 91

Creating Angles. Shakti Parwha Kaur Khalsa. 1996. *Kundalini Yoga: The Flow of Eternal Power.* The Berkley Publishing Company: New York. p. 241

The Power and Meaning of Sat Nam. Yogi Bhajan, Ph. D. 2007. The Aquarian Teacher: KRI International Kundalini Yoga Teacher Training Textbook Level One Instructor. Kundalini Research Institute: Santa Cruz, NM. p. 86

Eye Focus. Yogi Bhajan, Ph. D. 2007. *The Aquarian Teacher: KRI International Kundalini Yoga Teacher Training Textbook Level One Instructor. Kundalini Research Institute: Santa Cruz, NM. p. 136.*

Mudra insights. Yogi Bhajan, Ph. D. 2007. *The Aquarian Teacher: KRI International Kundalini Yoga Teacher Training Textbook Level One Instructor. Kundalini Research Institute: Santa Cruz, NM. p. 105*

Prayer Pose. Yogi Bhajan, Ph.D. 2007. *The Aquarian Teacher: KRI International Kundalini Yoga Teacher Training Textbook Level One Instructor.* Kundalini Research Institutue: Santa Cruz, NM. *p 105*

The Secrets Behind Prayer Pose. http://www.3ho.org/kundalini-yoga/mudra *Body Lock* insights. Yogi Bhajan, Ph. D. 2007. *The Aquarian Teacher: KRI International Kundalini Yoga Teacher Training Textbook Level One Instructor. Kundalini Rese*arch Institute: Santa Cruz, NM. *p. 107-11*

Tuning in. Guru Dharam S. Kaur Khalsa and Darryl O'Keefe. *2002. The Kundalini Yoga Experience: Bring Body, Mind and Spirit Together.* Simon and Schuster: New York. p. 53

Breath and Universe quote by Yogi Bhajan. Yogi Bhajan, 2011. *Success and the Spirit: An Aquarian Path to Abundance. Lectures and Meditations from the Teachings of Yogi Bhajan.* Kri Santa Cruz, NM. p. *199*

Sitali Pranayama. Yogi Bhajan, Ph.D. 2007. *The Aquarian Teacher: KRI International Kundalini Yoga Teacher Training Textbook Level One Instructor. Kundalini Research Institute: Santa Cruz*, NM. *p 97*

Sitali Pranayama [last two health benefits, and direct quote] from Yogi Bhajan. Yogi Bhajan. July 9, 1975. *Under The Blue Skies.* Kundalini Research Institute Publications [http://www. kundaliniresearchinstitute.org/tools4teachers/docs/Under_The_ Blue_Skies.pdf] p. 270

Spinal Twist. Guru Dharam S. Kaur Khalsa & Darryl O'Keefe. 2002. *The Kundalini Yoga Experience: Bring Body, Mind & Spirit Together. Simon and Schuster:* New York. p. 54; *Yogi Bhajan, Ph. D. 2007. The Aquarian Teacher: KRI International Kundalini Yoga Teacher Training Textbook Level One Instructor.* Kundalini Research Institute: Santa Cruz, NM. *. p. 320*

Miracle Bend. Yogi Bhajan. 2009. I Am Woman Creative Sacred and Invincible. Yogi Bhajan. The Kundalini Research Institute: Santa Cruz, NM. p.158

Siri Gaitri Mantra. Yogi Bhajan, Ph.D. 2007. *The Aquarian Teacher: KRI International Kundalini Yoga Teacher Training Textbook Level One Instructor.* Kundalini Research Institute: *Santa Cruz, NM.* pp. 178-179

Panj Shabd. Yogi Bhajan, *Ph.D. 2007. The Aquarian Teacher: KRI International Kundalini Yoga TeacherTraining Textbook Level One Instructor. Kundalini Research Institute:* Santa Cruz, NM, p. 87; *I Am Woman Creative Sacred and Invincible.* 2009. The Kundalini Research Institute. p.14

Divine Glands information. Shakti Parwha Kaur Khalsa . 1996. *Kundalini Yoga: The Flow of Eternal Power.* The Berkley Publishing Company: New York. p. 240

Addictions Meditation. Yogi Bhajan, Ph.D. 2007. *The Aquarian Teacher: KRI International Kundalini Yoga Teacher Training Textbook Level One Instructor. Kundalini Research Institute: Santa Cruz, NM.* p.109

The Last Resort [Depression]Meditation. Yogi Bhajan . 2009. *I Am Woman Creative Sacred and Invincible.* The Kundalini Research Institute: Santa Cruz, NM. p.110

The Three Minute Har Meditation. Yogi Bhajan . 2010. *The Aquarian Teacher: KRI International Kundalini Yoga Teacher Training Manual Level One Instructor.* Kundalini Research Institute: *Santa Cruz, NM.* P.113

Miracle Mantra. Yogi Bhajan, Ph.D. 2007. *The Aquarian Teacher: KRI International Kundalini Yoga Teacher Training Textbook Level One Instructor.* Kundalini Research Institute: *Santa Cruz, NM. p 82*

The Long Time Sun prayer. Yogi Bhajan . 2010. *Seeds of Change for the Aquarian Trasformation Volume One;Mastering the Self: 91 Transformational Kriyas and Meditations. Kundalini Research Institute. Santa Cruz, NM. On f*irst page after chapter outline of book.

I Am Bountiful, Blissful, and Beautiful quote by Yogi Bhajan. Yogi Bhajan. 2011. *Success and the Spirit: An Aquarian Path to Abundance: Lectures and Teachings of Yogi Bhajan.* Santa Cruz, NM. p. 23

About The Author

As a dedicated life student, spiritual seeker, energy healer, Registered Nurse, BScN, women's health educator, past teacher in Nursing to both university and college students, a student and teacher of Kundalini Yoga, and a mother of six beautiful daughters, Cindy has inspired and healed many over her 25 years as a practitioner in the medical field. Awarded for her *caring* in her nursing practice, she trail-blazes a sacred path that gives women permission to love themselves,  embrace their own greatness, and dare to believe in a power they own scientifically and energetically to raise their lives up to the level where magic and miracles live! This experience is called, living and being REAL Beautiful. In this book, Cindy uplifts women to higher levels of vibrational energy with some unique and powerful scientific practices that will help them feel *good enough* (in a society that steals this away), and come to know the honor and reverence they deserve in life. Cindy shares her spiritual journey filled with higher insights and her own near-death experience to help guide women to know themselves better as *energy beings* so they can create their own beauty, power, healing, happiness, success, heaven and more—the magic and miracles of life!

Get connected to the REAL Beautiful Movement and the beautiful secrets hidden inside your body at *www.realbeautiful.ca*. Learn more about the secret power of the mantra card on Cindy's website, and learn about the extra secret hidden gift it contains somewhere inside the pages of this book! Sign up for free gifts, personal counseling, a REAL Beautiful 40 Day Sacred Sadhana, a REAL Beautiful Retreat, download the upcoming Self-Love and Gratitude app, and so much MORE!